Praise for *Seizing the White Space*

"Companies which introduce new business models to their industry are able to take advantage of enormous opportunities. In *Seizing the White Space*, Johnson gives businesses the critical tools they need to develop new ways of bringing value to customers—and to make those opportunities a reality."

—Reed Hastings, founder and CEO, Netflix

"Bringing innovations successfully to market is as much about leadership as technical prowess. Mark Johnson has taken innovation out of the R&D lab and put it squarely where it belongs—in the executive suite. Any leader looking for growth from innovation will find new insights and practical tools in this book."

—Susan Marcinelli, Senior Vice President,
Innovation and Leadership Development, Best Buy

"Raising the ambitions of companies and leaders is the key to making any business model transformation process work. Johnson provides unique examples and insights that will make you think in new ways. A must-read."

—Arkadi Kuhlmann, President and CEO,
ING Direct, and coauthor, *The Orange Code*

"I know from my own experience how difficult it is to build a new business model within an established organization, where it is hard to shed the traditional mores and structures to effect real change. It would have been great to have Johnson's book—*Seizing the White Space* will be a valuable tool for anyone who wants to reshape a business."

—Bill Hambrecht, Chairman, WR Hambrecht + Co.

Seizing the
White Space

Seizing the White Space

Business Model Innovation for Growth and Renewal

Mark W. Johnson

Harvard Business Press
Boston, Massachusetts

Library of Congress Cataloging-in-Publication Data

Johnson, Mark W.
  Seizing the white space: business model innovation through growth and
renewal/Mark W. Johnson
      p. cm.
  ISBN 978-1-4221-2481-9 (hbk. : alk. paper)   1. Diversification in industry—
Management.   2. Business planning.   3. New products.   I. title.
  HD2756.J64 2010
  658.4'063—dc22

                                                                    2009033701

The paper used in this publication meets the requirements of the American
National Standard for Permanence of Paper for Publications and Documents in
Libraries and Archives Z39.48-1992.

For my mother, Adriana, who taught me by

example all the important things

And for my beloved wife, Jane, and my children,

Kristina, Mark, Kathryn, Ella, and William.

They remind me every day what matters most

The shift from oral to written speech is essentially a shift from sound to visual space . . . Because print controlled not only what words were put down to form a text but also the exact situation of the words on the page and their spatial relationship to one another, the space itself on a printed sheet—"white space" as it is called—took on high significance that leads directly into the modern and post-modern world.

—Walter Ong

CONTENTS

Part Three

Business Model Innovation as a Repeatable Process

FOREWORD

Since its beginning as a partnership between a candle maker and a soap manufacturer in 1837, Procter & Gamble has been a product innovator. Ivory ("the soap that floats") was invented in 1879; Dreft, the first synthetic laundry detergent, in the depths of the Depression in 1933; Tide, the first heavy-duty laundry detergent, in 1946; Crest, the first ADA-approved fluoride toothpaste, in 1955. Pampers, the first disposable diaper, was introduced in 1961; Pert Plus, the first combined shampoo and conditioner, in 1986; the Febreze fabric freshener and Swiffer mop in 1998; Crest Whitestrips, the first mass-market in-home tooth-whitening system, in 2001.

So it's not surprising that most people think the secret to P&G's success has been steady product innovation. But to grow on the scale that P&G does for as long as we have requires more than steady growth in core markets. It requires changes to what Mark Johnson calls in this book "something more core than core." It requires innovation in P&G's basic business models—that is, changes to the way we turn a profit, to the value propositions we offer our customers, to the way we combine our internal and external processes to go to market. Innovations like those we made in 1919, when we hired 450 sales representatives to sell directly to retailers rather than through wholesalers; or in 1924, when we set up the first market research department to understand changing trends in consumer demand; or in 1931, when we introduced the notion of fielding competing brands in the same category; or today, as we move into high-frequency stores in developing countries.

Over its history, in fact, P&G has reinvented itself about once a decade to respond to changes in consumer and market realities and to tackle barriers to realizing transformational growth opportunities. Innovation was among my top priorities during the nine years I served as P&G's CEO, and it remains a critical priority for Bob McDonald, who succeeded me. Over the course of my career, I've come to see business model innovation not as a static process but as a systemic, repeatable, and reliable capability, one that leaders need to build, strengthen, and eventually turn into a sustainable competitive advantage.

But how? *Business model innovation* has become a popular buzz phrase in the business press and in academia in recent years. Yet to my mind, it is a topic that few people understand at any rigorous level, and as a result it's not being accorded the importance it should have in most corporate and business-unit strategy processes.

That's why this book is so welcome. In *Seizing the White Space*, Johnson lays out a compelling case for business model innovation as the catalyst for robust growth, both through transformation of existing markets—the "white space within" that every company has—and through the creation of tomorrow's new markets—"the white space beyond" that so many companies find so hard to venture into.

It is welcome because Johnson has done the hard work of distilling just what a business model consists of: His interdependent four-box business model framework is a powerful synthesis, built from careful study of companies spanning a wide range of industries.

Equally important is his insight into just how relative white space is. One company's white space is another's home turf. That was an insight we used to great advantage at P&G, for example as we expanded Swiffer—a core product for us—into totally new markets where it represents a fundamentally new business model for our competitors.

Johnson's model sheds light on two areas that I have seen derail the best of management's intentions to seize white space. I've known situations in which we could identify new customer value propositions but were late to market, and times when we had conceived innovative new profit models but failed to commercialize them successfully. We were unable to put the right resources, external partners, or internal activity systems into place for those types of discontinuous innovation opportunities.

Reinvention at that level requires first that you know what business you're in. The four-box model—customer value proposition, profit formula, key resources, and key processes—makes the sources of a business's current success explicit. By extension, it identifies which ones need to change if a company is to capitalize on a new opportunity. *Seizing the White Space* provides top executives and innovation leaders with a comprehensive but user-friendly approach to making new-value creation a consistent, repeatable process.

Seizing white space is hard. It requires looking at markets and customers in new ways. It requires an openness to experimentation and uncertainty. It requires a willingness to challenge and change those well-honed systems and models that made your enterprise successful in the first place.

In recent years, Procter & Gamble has pursued three clear growth strategies: continue to grow the core business with leading brands in big, growing retail markets; develop fast-growing, higher-margin global businesses; and grow disproportionately in developing markets. On the face of it, these strategies might look like simply staying the course for a large, packaged goods company. But delivering on those strategies required significant changes to the business model P&G had been operating under for decades.

It required that we open our approach to innovation. We were known for doing everything ourselves; now we are becoming perhaps equally famous for our "Connect and Develop" open innovation program. This new approach entailed significant process changes to our core R&D capabilities.

It also required us to think differently about the value proposition we offer to consumers. Consumer needs in the 1980s and 1990s could largely be satisfied by improving the performance and features of our products as we competed on the basis of functionality, something Johnson points out is common in early-stage markets. But markets in the consumer products industry developed in the same way that many in Johnson's analysis do: competitors' products improved, and we at P&G found the basis of competition shifting as consumers demanded more customized products delivered in more convenient ways. By 2000, we needed to reset the bar and focus on innovations that had an impact on all the ways consumers experience our products, from the first time they encounter them in the store, to when they take them home and use them, and on through their final disposition. We needed to shift to a more holistic approach to innovation that encompassed not just concept and performance but also changes in communication, design, packaging, and value.

And ultimately, we needed to move beyond product and technology to service, supply chain, and cost innovations. For example, success in reaching emerging-market consumers demanded that we compete in multiple price tiers, not just in the premium tiers where we had long been a leader. This meant rethinking supply chains to make our products dramatically more affordable to greater numbers of consumers—and to people who had never been consumers of P&G products.

These are not innovations that develop only in R&D labs. Nor are they always innovations that require wholesale change. But they are all innovations that start with a deep understanding of your current business model—and how well suited it may or may not be to new opportunities. A solid understanding of current capabilities, together with a systematic approach to analyzing the business model requirements of new opportunities—like the one outlined in the following pages—makes the hard work of mapping out the white space rational and manageable. It takes it out of the realm of inspiration and serendipity and anchors it firmly in the world of strategy and executive leadership.

Recognizing this, P&G has put in place new business creation units at the corporate and business unit levels charged with identifying and developing opportunities both adjacent to our core and well outside it—opportunities that require us to be as innovative with our business models as we are with our products. As Johnson recommends, we are funding these ventures with seed money that is being kept away from the core and staffing them with "black belts" equipped with the best practices.

Johnson's architecture fits the real world strategies Procter & Gamble is working to create. His model reveals in a practical fashion those elements that we have learned through practice are essential to discontinuous innovation. As Johnson suggests, *Seizing the White Space* is the playbook you would want to take with you as you seek to conquer the unknown.

—A.G. Lafley
Chairman of the Board, Procter & Gamble,
Cincinnati, Ohio
September 2009

Part One

A New Model for Growth and Renewal

1

The White Space and Business Model Innovation

He who moves not forward, goes backward.

—Goethe

If you happened to be driving past a certain desolate airstrip in Palmdale, California, one January day in 2006 and glanced out your window, you would have seen something extraordinary on that bright, sunny morning—a large, dirigible-type aircraft floating down the runway.[1] Unlike most blimps, however, this one resembled three puffy hot dogs strapped together and mounted on four round pillows—a floating version, if you will, of the Oscar Mayer Weinermobile—with large swinging fans protruding from each side and the rear.

Pulling your vehicle off the road, you would likely have watched in amazement as this strange craft bounced and bumped down the short runway, rose from the ground, and climbed to about four hundred feet. Then, as its fans swung into action, you would have seen the craft glide into a long gentle bank, turn back parallel to the airstrip, and cruise down its length, and watched it bank gracefully again at the other end, fly in nose-first for a landing, and level off before gently touching down on its four hovercraft-like pads.

FIGURE 1

The Lockheed Martin P-791 hybrid airship

Photographs by Bob Driver and Gerhard Plomitzer

Palmdale, California, is a high desert community northeast of Los Angeles, a typical exurban sprawl of a major western city. Local residents know that the famed Skunk Works R&D division of aerospace giant Lockheed Martin often uses this airstrip as a proving ground for experimental projects. Had you been there that day, you would have borne witness to the first test flight of the Lockheed Martin P-791, a cross between a lighter-than-air dirigible and an airplane, a craft generically known as a hybrid airship. Unlike a blimp, which is truly lighter than air, a hybrid airship is a partially buoyant craft that combines the aerostatic lift of its gas-filled body with the aerodynamic lift supplied by its winglike shape and forward propulsion to achieve flight.

As lumbering as it appears, the hybrid airship can do two very valuable things exceedingly well. First, it can take off and land in a relatively small, unimproved space. Because it floats above the ground, it needs no runway in the conventional sense; it doesn't even require a smooth landing surface. Second, at full scale a hybrid airship can carry a very large payload, much larger than a helicopter or other short-takeoff and -landing aircraft.[2]

As word of the successful flight spread, Lockheed Martin found itself fielding inquiries from a host of potential commercial customers for a product it had not yet decided to make. Lockheed Martin's management quickly realized there could be a large market for this unique aircraft. Its introduction might represent a game-changing advance in air cargo and generate substantial new growth for the company. Mining companies that want to extract valuable ore from remote locations, for instance, are often thwarted by the cost of transporting heavy extraction machinery to the sites. A hybrid airship could simply float the machinery in. In places like India, where poor road infrastructure inhibits reliable truck transport, packaged-goods manufacturers could use a hybrid airship to move large quantities of their products to previously inaccessible areas. Fast-forward four years, however, and despite the seemingly huge upside, the P-791 hybrid airship is still not a commercialized product. Why? Technologically for Lockheed Martin, the hybrid airship should be a slam dunk. After all, this is the same company that delivered the storied F-117 Nighthawk stealth fighter, the F-16 Fighting Falcon, and the F-35 Lightning II joint strike fighter. Perhaps technical obstacles remain or the financial hurdles are too steep—only Lockheed Martin knows. But then again, maybe there's more to the story of why the hybrid airship project can't get off the ground.

VENTURING INTO THE WHITE SPACE

For decades, businesses of all stripes have wrestled with, failed to capitalize on, or passed over unique growth opportunities that did not seem to fit with what they already do well. Just think of Xerox's Palo Alto Research Center (PARC), which famously owned the technologies that helped catapult Apple, Adobe, and 3Com to success. Why didn't Xerox exploit them? More broadly, what underlying forces prevent great companies from embracing transformational opportunities?

Before we can answer that question, we must first understand something about where and how businesses tend to spend their time and resources in pursuit of new growth. At its most basic level, a company exists to deliver value in return for compensation. Every functioning company has a discrete sphere of operation—the activities it performs to serve a customer and in return make a profit. Early in a company's life, this space may resemble an inkblot without any logical boundaries flowing tentatively along paths of least resistance. As a company matures, its operations become better defined, its borders more clearly established. Company efforts and capabilities become concentrated on this *core operating space*.

Over time, a successful company becomes very good at growing its core. It secures resources, improves existing products and creates new ones, expands markets, and increases efficiencies by improving processes, all to extract the most value from its core activities. It also continues to develop and refine the key business rules and metrics that ensure proper execution, establish discipline, and exert control throughout the organization. Either explicitly or implicitly, the company is operating according to a *business model*, which defines the way the company delivers value to a set of customers at a profit. Like a highly specialized organism, this model evolves until it perfectly suits the company's needs—showcasing its competitive strengths, honing its key resources and processes, and eliminating its vulnerabilities.

But what happens when an opportunity arises outside a company's core, an opportunity to serve a wholly new customer or an existing customer in a radically new way? What happens when an opportunity arises to create an entirely new market or to significantly transform an existing one? What of challenging new growth opportunities like the P-791?

Many of these opportunities—even those that appear at first glance very different from the traditional core opportunity—fit quite well with the company's existing business model and thus are often called *adjacencies*. But some require a company to operate in a fundamentally different way—with a different formula for making money, a new set of resources and processes, different expertise, and maybe a new way to coordinate and control activities. When this occurs—when delivering new value to the market requires you to reconsider the fundamental building blocks that make the business work—that opportunity lies in your company's *white space*.

The term *white space* has been used in business parlance to mean uncharted territory or an underserved market. But what I mean by the term is *the range of potential activities not defined or addressed by the company's current business model, that is, the opportunities outside its core and beyond its adjacencies that require a different business model to exploit.* White space is a subjective valuation: one company's white space may be another company's

FIGURE 2

Defining the white space

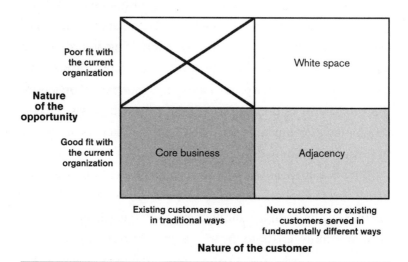

core. What matters is that it describes activities that lie far outside a firm's usual way of working and presents a series of unique and perplexing challenges to that organization. It's an area where, relatively speaking, assumptions are high and knowledge is low, the opposite of conditions in the company's core space.

The chance to seize a piece of white space presents a tantalizing opportunity. Success here can bring the transformational growth that so many business leaders seek. Yet understandably, a play for the white space feels risky, and often the numbers don't appear to add up. The market seems too foreign, or core capabilities won't apply. Some executives, having made one unsuccessful foray, just won't risk failing again.

LOCKHEED MARTIN'S WHITE SPACE

From Lockheed Martin's perspective, the commercial application of the P-791 hybrid airship lies far out in the white space. Lockheed Martin's core operating space is the relatively low-volume, high-margin world of multimillion-dollar fighter aircraft, missiles, space satellites, and specialized integrated-systems work. From its beginning as a naval and airframe maker in the early part of the twentieth century, Lockheed (Lockheed Martin after it merged with Martin Marietta in 1995) has served government customers using government contracting systems. It excels at delivering extremely complex solutions in a highly structured way to a small number of clients. Everything it makes is built to order, and every step in the process—from systems development to safety testing to aircraft assembly—is tracked and billed against detailed requirements or specifications, which means that margins are well defined in advance. Moreover, the defense industry's labyrinthine procurement process creates an effective barrier to entry for new rivals. As a result, Lockheed Martin occupies a relatively safe niche and therefore has little incentive to stake out new territory. Sticking to its knitting has been a successful formula so far: everything Lockheed Martin does fits into four specialized business units—Aeronautics (military aircraft), Electronic Systems (military electronics and system integration), Information Systems & Global Services (U.S. federal IT services), and Space Systems. Advanced Development Programs (ADP), as the Skunk Works is called today, is part of the Aeronautics unit. It develops advanced technologies and early prototypes, most of which are funded by the U.S. government.

The P-791 as a commercial product is in an entirely new, and far more mercurial, market space for Lockheed Martin. The company is accustomed to accurately projecting its products' potential markets, but since nothing like the P-791 has been built before, few existing metrics or market studies can predict its success. Making a significant investment in a product whose potential market size is merely assumed to be large seems irrational—especially since Lockheed Martin would probably have to shoulder the entire risk without government contract guarantees. Although comfortable with some types of uncertainty, the company has no existing processes for reducing the uncertainty of an unknown market.

Ironically, the very factors that signal the size of the opportunity are causes for concern in Lockheed Martin's world. To sell to the variety of customers who expressed interest in the P-791, it would need a wide range of new capabilities, including a commercial sales force and distribution channels, comfort and expertise operating in various cultures (mining, automotive, shipping, and the like), and a variety of marketing skills to reach multiple markets. Because commercial clients demand individual attention and each industry requires slightly different solutions, Lockheed Martin would also need to design a customizable offering, a far cry from its typically well-defined, fully specified military product. Finally, commercial ventures call for a completely different approach to managing finances, one that shares little with the government accounting standards, profit margins, and cash flow that drive the rest of Lockheed Martin's operations.

These are the challenges—all legitimate and noteworthy—that confronted Lockheed Martin when the P-791 hybrid airship floated out of its hangar in Palmdale that sunny day in 2006. When the ship lumbered slowly down the runway and its Oscar Mayer body bore it gently into the sky, it lifted off into Lockheed Martin's white space, a very scary place to fly.

ACHIEVING SUSTAINED GROWTH

Former Lockheed Martin chairman and CEO Norm Augustine once joked, "When it comes to diversification, the defense industry's record is unblemished by success."[3] While the hybrid airship clearly represents a thrilling opportunity for potentially transformational growth, that opportunity just as clearly lies many nautical miles from Lockheed Martin's core operating space. If you were Lockheed Martin, then, what would you do? Continue to target your existing customers or take the risk of going where so many have failed before?

This is an untenable choice that no CEO should have to make. To decide never to go into the white space is to make up your mind that your company will walk away from many of the opportunities it contains—that you will miss chances to transform an existing market, create a new one, or otherwise change the game in a powerful way to address competitors, disruptors, and industry discontinuities. Deciding never to venture into the white space leaves you with only your core and adjacencies to fuel your company's growth indefinitely.

Is that in any way realistic?

If ever there was a time that a business could just execute year after year and achieve lasting success, it is long gone. Notwithstanding economic contractions or crises as large as the financial collapse of 2008, the expectations of corporate stakeholders drive executives to plan for future growth even as they batten down the hatches and try to ride out the storm. To be sure, businesses in their adolescent stage, when their products and systems are just maturing, and those companies that have just made innovative leaps can rely almost exclusively on growth from the core. They can then move to adjacencies, serving new customers or existing ones in different ways by leveraging the existing business model. They can go on for quite a while creating new products and services to deliver on their financial targets, improving their tested formulas, better serving their existing customers, and even finding and serving new ones. And when new market expansion slows down, process innovations can yield significant efficiencies and continued growth.

But there comes a time when established product lines fully mature, when process innovation reaches the upper thresholds of efficiency, and when new product development slows. Then companies face a looming shortfall—a *growth gap*—between their desired growth path and the growth that the existing business

FIGURE 3

Defining the growth gap

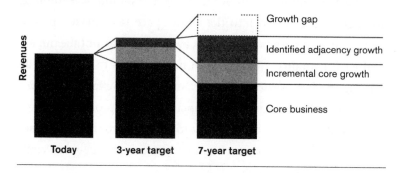

and envisioned adjacencies can deliver.[4] Commoditization, technological discontinuities, disruptive threats, changes in government policy or society's expectations, and intensified competition can all widen the growth gap, creating market conditions that significantly diminish the core's ability to grow.

Growth gaps are not new (although I would argue that they are arising faster and more frequently than ever before). Over the years, various business trends and management doctrines have emerged to address them. In the 1960s, many companies acquired undervalued but comparably sized companies in an attempt to buy growth. Although the rationale for conglomeration centered on the supposed benefits of scope of diversification, many of the acquisitions grew no faster—in fact, some grew more slowly—than before they were bought. Such attempts at growth amounted to little more than an accounting scheme, and when interest rates rose toward the end of the decade, most conglomerates were exposed for the bubble plays they were. With a few notable exceptions like General Electric, United Technologies, and Berkshire Hathaway, the majority of conglomerates lost value. And by the mid-1970s, most had been broken up or greatly diminished.

In the late 1970s and early 1980s, companies seeking growth created tightly defined businesses that grew by expanding on their core expertise. Acquisitions were judged by how well they complemented the core. When growth from the core proved insufficient to meet the pressure for new growth, management thinking expanded again. Companies could grow through adjacencies.[5]

But as successful as the strategy of growth from the core and adjacencies has been in building solid, well-integrated businesses, it's a strategy that forgoes the white space, assuming defeat from the outset.

Perhaps Lockheed Martin still has that luxury. Perhaps not. But certainly organizations in a multitude of fields—from media to health care to finance to energy to automotive to education to national defense—do not. These companies need something more fundamental than new growth: They need *renewal*. They must evolve into companies that deliver new sorts of value. And that means leaving the comfort of their core and pursuing opportunities in their white space. Seizing the white space requires new skills, new strengths, new ways to make money. It calls for the ability to innovate something more core than the core, to innovate the very theory of the business itself. I call that process *business model innovation*.

THE iPOD COMETH

One company that found this out (perhaps inadvertently) was Apple. Once a major player in the personal computer market, Apple watched its market share fall from 20 percent to less than 3 percent in the 1990s.[6] After struggling for years, during which the company settled into the role of a niche player, cofounder Steve Jobs returned from the business desert (where he'd been building a silly little company called Pixar). He was determined to put things right at Apple.

To refloat the sinking ship, he followed the well-trodden path of product innovation, quickly rolling out the iMac (whose fashion-forward industrial design integrated the processor with the monitor) and the iBook low-end laptop. He also made sure that suppliers like Microsoft and Adobe continued to develop software for Apple. The new products were by all accounts smash hits, but they did little more than stop the bleeding. You probably believe you know what happened next: in 2001, Apple introduced the iPod, the world's first digital music player, a product that revolutionized the way we consume portable entertainment, created an entirely new market, and set Apple on the road to exponential growth. Jobs and his team pulled off a triumph of product development that changed the rules of the game.

Except that *isn't* what happened. Apple was not, in fact, the first company to bring a digital music player to market; that honor belongs to Diamond Media, which introduced the first MP3 player, the Rio, in 1998. Another company, Best Data, introduced its version, the Cabo 64, in 2000.[7] So why did Apple's iPod revolutionize the music world? Was Apple's product better? Was its design more elegant? Well, those factors undoubtedly influenced consumers, but Diamond's and Best Data's products were also functional, portable, and stylish. In fact, the original iPod looked very much like the Rio's dial-controlled design.

Apple did something far smarter than wrap a good technology in a snazzy design; *it wrapped a good technology in a great business model.* Apple's genius lay in its realization that making it easy and convenient to download music to the iPod would fuel demand for its high-priced music player. Eighteen months after introducing the iPod, Apple launched the iTunes Store, a service component that tightly locked hardware, software, and digital music into one user-friendly package. This move recalled one of the great business model innovations of all time: King Gillette revolutionizing men's shaving by choosing to give away the razor handle—a durable—in order to lock customers in to purchasing his consumable, high-margin blades. Apple reversed Gillette's model, essentially giving away the blades—low-margin, consumable iTunes music—to lock in the purchase of the handle—the iPod—whose high margin returned high profits.[8]

This business model, substantially different from anything Apple had done before, defined value in a new way. The success of this business model innovation rejuvenated—indeed transformed—Apple. In just three years, the iPod/iTunes combination became a $10 billion product, accounting for nearly 50 percent of the company's revenue. Apple's market capitalization skyrocketed from around $2.6 billion at the end of 2002 to $133 billion at the end of 2007, during the key years of the iPod/iTunes' growth.[9] What's more, its digital platform became the basis of a newly defined Apple

FIGURE 4

The impact of iPod/iTunes on Apple's growth

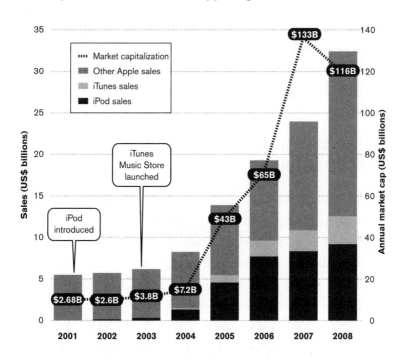

Note: Market cap figures represent data for the end of the fiscal year.
Source: Apple 10k 2003–2008; Yahoo Finance; Innosight analysis.

brand. No longer was Apple simply one competitor among many in the rapidly commoditizing PC hardware space. It became a leader in the world of lifestyle media. Its new business model has paved the way for further evolution, as Apple subsequently moved into video content and convergent media.

It would be easy to think that the iPod was a natural fit for Apple, a low-risk extension of its core hardware/software system–integration expertise. But it actually represented a white-space move. Apple had been a computer maker. It had limited experience with the world of music or media and virtually no identity in the public's mind as a provider of entertainment technology. Sony's Walkman line had dominated the portable music market since the early 1980s.[10] In fact, the music industry was deeply suspicious of MP3 technology, which it correctly thought would cannibalize the CD market. To enter hostile territory and propose an unproven technology with little or no track record in the space was risky indeed for Apple. It would have been impossible if Apple hadn't devoted as much creative energy to innovating its business model as it did its products.

SEIZING THE WHITE SPACE WITH BUSINESS MODEL INNOVATION

Business model innovations have already reshaped entire industries and redistributed billions of dollars of value. In retail, discounters like Target, Walmart, and Amazon that entered the market with innovative business models by 2007 accounted for 76 percent of the total industry market capitalization, having seized more than $300 billion of value. Low-fare U.S. discount and regional airlines grew from a blip on the radar screen to 55 percent of the market value of all carriers.[11] More than half of the twenty-six companies founded since 1984 that have entered

FIGURE 5

Business model innovation in U.S. retailing

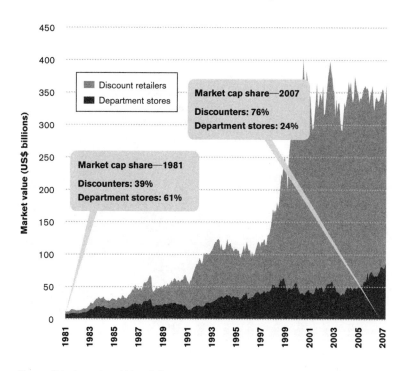

Source: Datastream; Innosight analysis.

the *Fortune* 500 between 1997 and 2007 did so through business model innovation.[12]

It's no wonder, then, that *business model innovation* is an executive buzz phrase. A 2008 IBM survey found that nearly all of the more than eleven hundred corporate CEOs polled reported the need to adapt their business models; more than two-thirds said that extensive changes were required.[13] Yet despite all the talk, few seem to know how to pull it off. No more than 10 percent of innovation investments at global companies are currently focused on developing new business models.[14] And the companies that do

FIGURE 6

Business model innovation in the U.S. airline industry

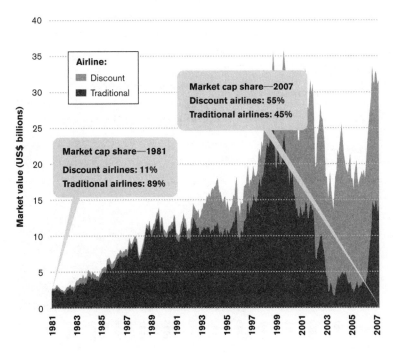

Source: Datastream; Innosight analysis.

attempt it rarely succeed—despite all the talent and resources at their disposal. Most successful innovative business models are forged by start-ups. Why doesn't this immense promise and high-level attention translate to action? Companies can't pull it off because, as familiar as the term is, very few people really understand what a business model is (and what it isn't) or what model their organization is actually operating under, much less how they would go about creating a new one and why or when they should.

The solution to this perplexing challenge lies in the pages ahead. In chapter 2, I define the elements of a successful business model and explain how they interrelate. Part II addresses market circumstances that open up opportunities and imperatives to

FIGURE 7

Companies founded since 1984 that have entered the *Fortune* 500 sometime between 1997 and 2007

Business model innovator	Description	Non-business model innovator	Description
Amazon.com	Operates retail Web sites. Receives early payment for merchandise transactions. Makes low margins on high turnover of stock.	**AGCO**	Manufactures and distributes agricultural equipment and related replacement parts.
AutoNation	Automotive retailer offers no-haggle pricing and transparent financing on all vehicles.	**Allied Waste Industries**	Waste management company that provides various services to customers. Serves high share of market.
BJ's Wholesale Club	Warehouse club operator offers customers access to merchandise in bulk through membership fees.	**Asbury Automotive Group**	Automotive dealer offers wide variety of products and services, following industry norms.
Blockbuster	Originated the movie rental market. Sells and rents games and movies.	**BorgWarner**	Global supplier of components for power train applications and engineered automotive systems.
CarMax	Sells used cars through no-haggle pricing. Makes the buying and selling of cars two separate activities.	**Charter Communications**	Broadband communications company that offers traditional cable, Internet, and telephone services.
Community Health Systems	Hospital operator provides health care services primarily in underserved, nonurban markets.	**Chesapeake Energy**	Producer and owner of oil and natural gas wells.
DaVita	Provides dialysis services for patients suffering from chronic kidney failure. Specialists operate in outpatient dialysis centers.	**Energy Transfer Equity**	Owns and operates transportation and storage businesses, numerous natural gas transportation pipelines, storage facilities, and treatment facilities.
eBay	Online marketplace with attendant payment services and forum for peer-to-peer online auctions.	**Group 1 Automotive**	Markets and sells a range of automotive products and services.
Express Scripts	Pharmacy benefit management company that specializes in processing and payment of prescription drug claims.	**NRG Energy**	Owns, develops, constructs, and operates power generation facilities.
GameStop	Retailer of video game products and software. Solicits used equipment to resell, then gives sellers store credit.	**Sonic Automotive**	Automotive retailer that operates large number of sales and maintenance dealerships.
Google	Maintains massive index of online content. Generates revenue through online advertising.	**United Auto Group**	Auto services company that engages in facilities management, maintenance, engineering, and construction.
Qualcomm	Wireless telecommunication company that generates large revenues by licensing its IP.	**XTO Energy**	Explores and develops oil and gas properties. Also produces, markets, and transports oil and natural gas.
Starbucks	Owns and operates large chain of hip coffee stores. Category killer that upended mom-and-pop coffee shops.		
Yahoo!	Major online navigational guide for the Web. Generates revenue by providing advertisers with marketing services.		

seize the white space through business model innovation. In it, I explore how business model innovation can empower organizations to transform existing markets, create new ones, or recast whole industries—and how new business models can deploy cutting-edge, enabling technologies for transformative growth. Finally, in Part III, I lay out in detail a structured process for designing new business models and developing them into profitable, thriving enterprises, and investigate the managerial challenges that commonly thwart unguided forays into the unknown.

With this book, you can turn business model innovation into a managed process and a more predictable discipline. When we're done, I hope that you will thoroughly understand how great business propositions are constructed and recognize that even the most traditional company can achieve transformational growth and renewal in its white space. To play a new game on a new field requires a new game plan. Business model innovation will give you a language and framework for understanding both the core space of your existing enterprise and the white space you hope to seize. Think of this as your playbook for conquering the unknown.

2

The Four-Box Business Model Framework

The structure of language determines not only thought but reality itself.

—Noam Chomsky

In his seminal book, *An Actor Prepares,* the great drama coach Konstantin Stanislavsky tells the story of an actor asked to hide under a table; according to a stage direction, an imminent threat was just offstage. An actor's job, of course, is to draw on his life experience to create real emotions and actions within the imagined confines of a script and a stage. This actor was trying to find the emotional motivation to dive under the table, but he could not convince himself that he was truly afraid. Unable to feel the fear, he couldn't perform.

Do not think, the master teacher told him, just dive under the table and cover your head. The actor did so. What do you feel? the teacher asked. I feel afraid, said the student. Sometimes you feel afraid and you dive under the table, the master concluded, but sometimes, if you dive under the table, you will feel afraid.[1] Stanislavsky's great contribution to Western art was to propose that while creative inspiration often leads to structure, just as often, structure unlocks creativity.

The same dynamic holds true for business model innovation. The main reason most companies fail at new business creation is that they fear to act without an unambiguous motive to do so. Staffed with people trained to operate within the defined norms of their company and their industry, they shy away from moves that don't immediately make sense within the context of their current operations. Like the actor who could not dive under the table unless it made emotional sense for him to do so, they resist venturing into the unknown territory of business model innovation when so much uncertainty clouds the path to success. Who knows what's under the table? And who is willing to risk his job to find out?

Occasionally, a visionary leader—a Jeff Bezos or a Steve Jobs— intuitively understands what it takes to innovate a business model or to build an entirely new one. The rest of us need an explicit framework and a manageable process to reduce the uncertainty and risk of venturing into the unknown. As Stanislavsky taught, we need structure to unlock our creativity—a disciplined process that can spur us toward new ideas. The better we understand the structure of business models, the better we will be at creating them.

A business model, in essence, is a representation of how a business creates and delivers value, both for the customer and the company. Of course, the notion of how value is created and delivered is fundamental, but strangely, businesses can rarely articulate it clearly. Most leaders don't sufficiently understand their company's existing business model, the premise behind its development, its natural interdependencies, or its strengths and weaknesses when in pursuit of new growth. They simply don't know if they should leverage their core business and established model to deliver on a new customer opportunity or if that proposition is a move into the white space requiring a new business model. Value remains curiously implicit, as if it were some guiding presence that hovers beneath the surface of the enterprise. Indeed, the consequent clumsiness in creating new business models has led to the widespread belief that companies can only successfully innovate close to the core.

Part of the problem is a lack of a shared vocabulary. Thought leaders in the past have offered numerous definitions of a business model. The late management guru Peter Drucker implicitly defined it as "the theory of the business."[2] Management consultant and author Joan Magretta described business models as "stories that explain how enterprises work."[3] Other management theorists and practitioners have devised frameworks, some of which focus purely on the economics of a business while others take an impossibly wide scope, including almost every aspect of business strategy and organization.[4] No one to my knowledge squarely focuses on the elements in the business system that are central to value's creation and delivery and the way those elements work together to ensure or impede the overall success of the enterprise.

To render the most essential elements of value creation in clear language, I propose a four-box business model framework. I believe it provides the structure needed to reveal and categorize all of the issues that must be addressed before a company can confidently venture into the low-knowledge, high-assumption environment of its white space. Employed methodically, the framework will give you a road map to new possibilities for innovation, transformational growth, and renewal that you never before thought you could capitalize on.

FIGURE 8

The four-box business model

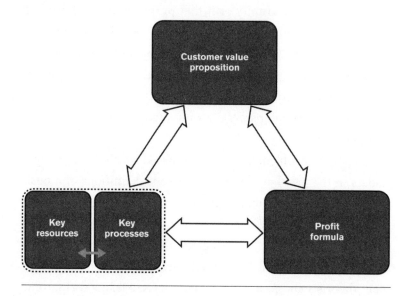

THE FOUR KEY ELEMENTS OF A BUSINESS MODEL

The basic architecture underlying all successful businesses consists of four interdependent elements that can be represented with four boxes. First, every thriving enterprise is propelled by a strong *customer value proposition* (CVP)—a product, service, or combination thereof that helps customers do more effectively, conveniently, or affordably a job that they've been trying to do. The CVP describes how a company creates value for a given set of customers at a given price. Second, the *profit formula* defines the way the company will capture value for itself and its shareholders in the form of profit. It distills the often-complex financial calculations into the four variables most critical to profit generation: revenue model, cost structure, target unit margin, and resource velocity. The third and fourth elements of the model, *key resources* and *key processes*, are the means by which the company delivers the value to the customer and itself. They are the critical assets, skills, activities, routines, and ways of working that enable the enterprise to fulfill the CVP and profit formula in a repeatable, scalable fashion.[5] When properly integrated together and congruent with the CVP and profit formula, they provide the essence of a company's competitive advantage. Every successful company is fulfilling a real customer job-to-be-done with an effective, well-integrated business model, whether it knows it or not.[6]

The power of this deceptively simple framework lies in the complex interdependencies of its parts. Successful businesses devise a relatively stable system in which these elements interact in consistent and complementary ways. A change to any one of the four affects all the others and the system as a whole. Incongruities or conflicts between elements, even seemingly inconsequential ones, can bring about its downfall.

Let's examine each element (or box) more closely with an eye toward revealing how each contributes to a powerful understanding of the dynamics and process of business model change.

CUSTOMER VALUE PROPOSITION (CVP)

> *Customer value proposition:* An offering that helps customers more effectively, reliably, conveniently, or affordably solve an important problem (or satisfy a job-to-be-done) at a given price.

A powerful, focused customer value proposition is the keystone of all successful business models. A great CVP identifies an important, unsatisfied consumer problem, or "job," and then proposes a focused product or service (or combination) to do that job at a given price. Before you can design a great CVP, you must first develop a comprehensive understanding of your target customer's job-to-be-done.

FIGURE 9

Customer value proposition (CVP)

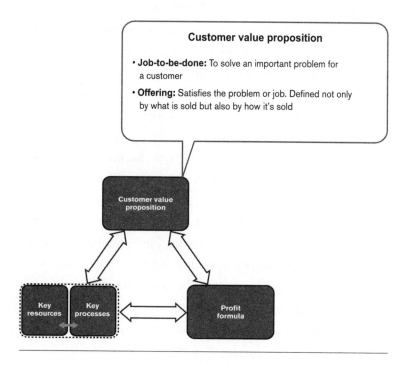

As Harvard Business School professor Theodore Levitt first pointed out, customers do not really buy products—they hire them to accomplish particular tasks.[7] He famously said that people don't go to the hardware store to buy a drill, for instance; they go to buy a hole. The drill they purchase is the candidate hired to get that job done.[8] Over the last few decades, a lot of emphasis has been put on "customer needs" and "the voice of the customer." But understanding a customer's job-to-be-done is not the same as understanding a customer. Too often, "needs" are defined too broadly or, worse, are thought of only in relation to existing products and services. To develop new CVPs in the white space, you must stop trying to figure out what kinds of products people are trying to buy and instead work out what they are trying to get done in their lives in a given circumstance.

To illustrate, let's consider the cell phone and its cousin, the smartphone. A cell phone addresses the job, "I want to conveniently make phone calls when I'm on the go, away from my home or office."[9] If you ask people why they chose a smartphone rather than a cell phone, most will say something like, "I don't just want to communicate; I also want to organize my life on the go." Because no other gadget performed these functions and satisfied this job-to-be-done, smartphones became very popular. Palm, Research in Motion (RIM) (maker of the BlackBerry), and other vendors built their businesses by providing better calendars, faster connections, and easier e-mail applications to address this job.

Now think about the last time you attended an overly long business meeting, had spare time in an airport between connections, or waited for your lunch at a restaurant. In those moments, your job-to-be-done was different: "Help me kill small snippets of time in useful ways." That job could be fulfilled by many means. You could read a magazine or newspaper, watch TV in the airport bar, listen to a recorded book, or scribble a memo. But maybe a smartphone could provide many more useful and more convenient alternatives—easily accessible stock quotes, say, or news headlines; games that you could play quickly; chat functions, Twitter access, and the like. This new job-to-be-done calls for a new customer value proposition, and the Apple iPhone—with a full Web browser and a host of downloadable applications to suit every taste—offered it, in the process redefining just how smart a smartphone could be.

Learning from its past success with the iPod, Apple again embraced a sales-and-service model and built the App Store, which hosts products from a diverse community of third-party developers. Competing for this second job-to-be-done changed the market for smartphones, and following Apple's success, RIM, Palm, and other competitors rushed to follow suit.

Identifying a critical job-to-be-done requires adopting a proactive, outside-in approach (which I will discuss in more detail in chapter 6), for as Peter Drucker noted, "The customer rarely buys what the company thinks it is selling him."[10] With effort, every job-to-be-done can be precisely defined and categorized.

Once you fully understand the various dimensions of the job-to-be-done, you can design an offering that fulfills that job in a unique way. An *offering* is a product, service, or some combination, made available at an affordable price. Included in the concept of an offering is the experience of purchasing, using, and maintaining it. Sometimes, for instance, a job can be satisfied more by *how* something is sold than by *what* is sold: The first plain-paper photocopier, the iconic Xerox 914, languished when it was introduced in the 1960s. Companies didn't want to pay a high price for an unproven technology. So Xerox president Joe Wilson borrowed an idea from IBM and offered to lease the machines instead, charging a per-copy usage fee.[11] Business skyrocketed.

The job-to-be-done and the offering combine to form the customer value proposition for any successful business model. The overall value of a successful CVP derives from three key metrics:

1. How important the job-to-be-done is to customers.

2. How satisfied customers are with current solutions.

3. How well the new offering gets the job done, relative to the other options.

The more important the job, the better the match between the job and the offering, and, generally, the lower the offering's price, the greater the overall value generated for the customer from the customer value proposition.[12]

Identifying important unfulfilled jobs—the first critical step in developing a new CVP—often requires close observation. Imagine, for a moment, you are standing on a hot and dusty street in New Delhi, watching the snarl of traffic. At first, you see only chaos, but soon you discern patterns in the pandemonium. You notice the many motor scooters snaking through gridlocked cars.

FIGURE 10

The customer value proposition formula

How do you maximize a CVP?	**1** Identify an important job-to-be-done that is poorly satisfied today for a customer	then	**2** Devise and develop an offering that does the job better than alternatives at the lowest appropriate price

As you look more closely, you see whole families—parents and children—perched precariously on a single scooter. You might think, "That's crazy!" or, "That's the way it is. People get by as best they can." You shake your head and go on.

When Ratan Tata, president and chairman of Tata Sons (the holding company of Tata Motors, a leading vehicle maker in India for more than fifty years), looked out over the same scene, he saw a national problem and recognized a critical job-to-be-done: "Get these families off scooters and into something safe." He knew that many families could not afford a car: the cheapest one available in India costs almost five times as much as a scooter. "What if I can change the game and make a car for Rs1 lakh [around US$2,000]?" Tata thought. Producing a car for that amount, about half the price of the cheapest car available, could improve millions of lives, he reasoned.[13] The car would reduce injuries and fatalities for "scooter families," not to mention protect them from the scorching sun. It was a powerful customer value proposition, one with the potential to reach tens of millions of nonconsumers.

In April 2009, Tata's Rs1-lakh car, the Tata Nano, became available for pre-sale. In just one month, Tata's Web site garnered 30 million hits, showrooms welcomed 1.4 million visitors, and buyers put down deposits of as much as 80 percent on more than 200,000 cars (equivalent to 17 percent of the annual new car market in India).[14]

At the other end of the market and the other side of the world, John Mackey, cofounder and CEO of natural foods retailer Whole Foods Market, looked out on a different sort of street, one traveled by relatively well-off food aficionados, middle-aged baby boomers grown increasingly conscious of their health, shoppers interested in sustainable consumption, and health-food consumers. Like Ratan Tata, Mackey discerned in this traffic jam of disparate general-merchandise customers an unserved job-to-be-done. These otherwise unconnected consumer groups all wanted a very high grade of fresh perishables—organic produce, cruelty-free meat, wild-caught fish, and the like—not widely available in local supermarkets. They wanted to live healthier, tastier, and more sustainable lives, but most lacked access to the scattered farmers' markets and specialty stores that could make that possible. Available solutions were not good enough to serve their job-to-be-done.

At the time, Whole Foods was one of those small providers, a regional chain of health-food stores that catered to the naturopathic-conscious consumer niche. Mackey believed that if Whole Foods could furnish a superior grade of perishables, then the much larger group of food connoisseurs and green buyers would also find Whole Foods' core natural and naturopathic products appealing. Making the supermarket consumption experience more pleasurable would further add to the appeal.

So Whole Foods reached out from its crunchy granola core to serve a customer looking for the focused job: "Give me full and pleasurable access to a variety of foods and products that meet my high standards for quality and honor my interests in health, organics, and protecting the environment."[15] It built a customer value proposition to address a job-to-be-done for which high-end consumers were willing to pay a premium.

Simplicity and elegance drive the formulation of great CVPs. Their power lies in their clarity, but clarity can be difficult to achieve. All too often, rather than focusing on a single job, companies attempt to fulfill many jobs at once. In doing lots of things, they do nothing very well.

Focused CVPs are as important for what they rule out as for what they rule in. By concentrating on jobs, a well-defined CVP helps overenthusiastic innovators resist the temptation to overload offerings with features that customers don't want to buy (and will resent paying for).

If you can't describe your customer value proposition in a few sentences that non-businesspeople can understand, then it is not clear or focused enough. Focused CVPs yield focused new business models, and a well-defined new business model allows incumbents to better understand when they need to replace their existing model to reach new target customers.

PROFIT FORMULA

Profit formula: *The economic blueprint that defines how the company will create value for itself and its shareholders. It specifies the assets and fixed cost structure, as well as the margins and velocity required to cover them.*

What revolutionizes industries are not powerful ways to make money per se but powerful customer value propositions that require money to be made in revolutionary ways. The profit formula defines the gross and net margins the organization must achieve, given the structure and magnitude of the fixed and variable costs inherent in its resources. It specifies how big the organization must become in order to break even and the pattern of profit improvement, if any, that comes with increasing scale. And the profit formula defines how fast the organization must turn over its assets to achieve adequate returns. In retailing, for example, companies like R.H. Macy and Federated Department Stores found success with a high-touch customer value proposition whose profit formula involved high markups and low inventory turns. When catalog companies like Sears came along, their profit formulas entailed a lower markup, but they could turn inventory much faster to make similar aggregate profits. Then a major revolution started in the 1950s with the emergence of discount retailers like E.J. Korvette and Zayre in the northeast United States, then Aldi in Germany, and eventually Kmart and Target throughout the

FIGURE 11

Profit formula

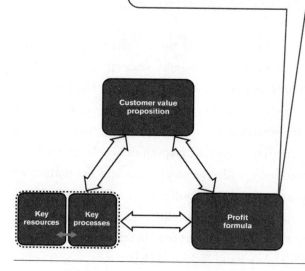

United States. To offer lower prices than department stores and mail-order houses, discount retailers needed to lower the markup on their merchandise even further. To do that and still make a profit, they needed to generate higher inventory turns—in other words, move more product more quickly through their stores.

The discount retailers initially achieved a lower overall cost structure by focusing on hard goods that "sell themselves," which enabled the discounters to substantially reduce one of the highest costs in retailing—service personnel.[16] Then discount retailing went even further when it went online. Companies such as Amazon were able to generate profits with even less of a markup by turning inventory even faster.

Interestingly, since Amazon dramatically improved the speed at which inventory moved through its system, it also maximized the return from its working capital. And it shifted the cash flow from a seller-financed model to a buyer-financed one.[17]

Before Amazon, book retailers paid publishers for merchandise 90 days after they received it but on average held it in inventory

FIGURE 12

Shifting profit formulas in the retailing industry

	Department stores	Catalog retailers	Discount retailers	Online-only retailers
Average markup over cost of inventory	40%	30%	23%	5%
Inventory turns	3x	4x	5x	25x
Return of inventory invested (markup × inventory turns)	120%	120%	115%	125%

Source: Clayton Christensen and Richard S. Tedlow, "Patterns of Disruption in Retailing," Harvard Business Review, January–February 2000, 42–45.

for 168 days, essentially carrying the cost of the product for 78 days. Combining Internet technology with just-in-time supply chain management, Amazon changed that fundamental dynamic, turning inventory much faster and reducing overhead even more. Instead of 168 days, Amazon held a book in inventory an average of just 17 days.[18] Even though Amazon agreed to pay publishers sooner than the industry standard—in about 58 days—its profit formula created a float that kept the customer's money in its hands for an average of 41 days. Doing so enabled Amazon to survive while e-tailing was still a relatively low-volume channel and then to thrive as the sector achieved scale.

I've identified four variables that I believe are the key determinants of a successful profit formula. These variables are tightly interrelated and work together to clearly define ways value can be created for the company and its shareholders, and are therefore critical to predicting the success of a new business model.

Revenue Model

The *revenue model* is the offering price times the quantity sold. The profit formula is tightly linked to, and significantly defined by, the customer value proposition because the offering price is an essential part of both. In the CVP, the offering price is a key quantifier of value. Its role in the profit formula depends on whether the company is devising a low-end or a premium business. In low-cost business models, price is a key starting point for determining the profit formula. Tata had little choice but to sell the Nano for Rs1 lakh if it wanted to deliver its value proposition of a safer vehicle for scooter families. In premium businesses, the price tends to be dictated by the cost of the resources needed to deliver the CVP. Whole Foods, for instance, knew that it needed to offer a superior grade of perishables to deliver on its CVP, which led it to devise a profit formula that involved higher-end pricing.

FIGURE 13

Amazon versus traditional book retailer

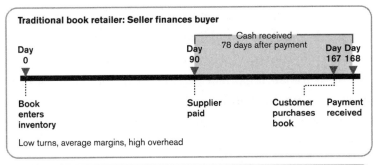

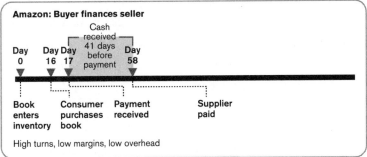

Source: William A. Sahlman and Laurence E. Katz, "Amazon.com—Going Public,"
Case 9-899-033 (Boston: Harvard Business School Publishing, 1998), 22.

The second half of the equation—quantity (or volume)—can be measured in various ways, such as market share or projected sales. Service businesses typically measure it as the time taken to perform a service or the number of transactions; manufacturers generally use quantity sold. A comprehensive approach to defining quantity asks three questions:

1. How many customers will I have?

2. How many units per customer per transaction will I sell?

3. How many transactions per customer can I expect?

The first question goes to the potential of the customer addressed by the CVP. The other two define the type of offering developed to satisfy the job-to-be-done.

A futher question you should consider in this connection is, How much additional income can I project from related products or services? It isn't strictly a part of the cost structure of the offering, but it has an important bearing on its long-term success. Apple, for example, controls nearly 70 percent of the MP3 player market and, as the market reaches saturation, anticipates declining sales.[19] Owing to recent song price increases, however, its ancillary income from music sales is still in sharp ascent. In fact, Apple recently passed Walmart to become the largest music seller in the world, with revenues approaching $1 billion.[20] Its revenue model includes a mechanism for ancillary income designed to compensate for eventual declining iPod sales.

Cost Structure

The *cost structure* is simply made up of direct costs and overhead, taking into account economies of scale. Successful companies typically have well-defined cost structures, and overhead requirements in particular are very difficult to change. So there's a strong impulse to start with existing overhead costs when devising the cost structure of a new business model. But that order is backwards; in the new model, the overhead must be determined by the requirements of the value proposition, not taken as a given.

Target Unit Margin

The *target unit margin* is the operating profit per unit required to cover overhead costs and achieve the desired profit level at the target volume. Strictly speaking, it's an outgrowth of the revenue model and the cost structure, but I call it out here separately because it's used so often in many companies as a proxy for the entire profit formula. Looking at margins in isolation and fear that a new business model's margins will be too low are the chief factors preventing incumbents from developing transformational growth opportunities. Smaller margins look to many companies' strategists and finance people like a threat to the viability of the firm, insufficient to cover the overhead. So they are usually quick to block initiatives that don't meet the margins of the core business model. But margins are only part of an overall profit formula—the goal is not necessarily to maintain any certain margin but to achieve the margin needed to reap the target profits.

Resource Velocity

Resource velocity defines how quickly resources need to be used to support target volume. It specifies not just the number of widgets a business can make, but how many it can invent, design, produce, warehouse, ship, service, sell, and pay for throughout the value chain for a given amount of investment during a given amount of time. Similar to asset turnover, this variable includes not only the actual turnover of current assets like inventory but the ability of the overhead or other related resources and established processes to support the planned turnover. This is an extremely important factor that, as Amazon's example demonstrates, is often overlooked.

Resource velocity is the answer to the question, How will volume production be achieved? It determines the overall capacity of the entire business model to serve the CVP. The greater the resource velocity of a business, the greater volume of its offering the business can produce. Innovations that increase resource velocity allow you to make acceptable aggregate profits at lower gross-unit margins.

Like overhead in the cost structure, resource velocity tends to be very rigid in existing business models. Everything from floor space to the physical proximity of parts to the production line to overhead operations has been carefully planned out and tends to be taken as immutable, leading incumbents to unnecessarily (and sometimes fatally) limit their horizons when considering the feasibility of new opportunities, since those designs may not work for a new CVP. Too often when that happens, companies reject the new CVP rather than explore the possibility of constructing a comprehensive new business model that would make it profitable.

Each element in a profit formula profoundly influences the others. For example, Ratan Tata knew that drastically decreasing the price of the product required accepting a sharp reduction in gross-unit margins and engineering a concurrent reduction in the full cost structure, lower than any car company had ever before achieved. Classic business economics told him, however, that he could still make an overall profit on lower gross-unit profit margins if he could increase resource velocity and thus sales volume.[21]

For Whole Foods, the key to profitability lay in shifting more of its sales volume to areas of the store that produced higher margins. The traditional revenue-generating, high-volume areas of supermarkets are the center aisles. Most markets offer perishables— vegetables, milk, meat, and cheese—at low margins to attract customers, banking that they will also buy large amounts of the more profitable dry goods and supplies. Whole Foods' target customers, by contrast, are willing to pay higher prices for high-quality, often organic, fresh perishables and prepared foods, shifting volume and much of the profitability to the periphery of the store.[22] Although they also want the natural and organic dry goods, Whole Foods' customers purchase far fewer of these items than they would in a nonspecialty supermarket.

Mainstream supermarkets keep costs low through a system of highly organized central distribution networks. Natural food suppliers, by contrast, tend to be small, local producers. Whole Foods' higher direct food costs, greater management complexity, and the need to coordinate numerous, low-volume suppliers adds up to high overhead costs. Selling more perishables and prepared foods and fewer commodity items means lower overall inventory turns, furthering the need for greater markup overall.

Essentially, Whole Foods inverted the established supermarket model. It relies not on volume but on higher prices and higher margins on the perishables, which its customers buy in large quantities.[23] To sell customers on higher prices, it invests heavily in making the grocery-shopping experience more pleasurable and less tiresome. By considering the customer experience an integral part of its CVP and devising the appropriate profit formula to satisfy it, Whole Foods commands the higher margins it needs to satisfy its customers' job-to-be-done. People often believe a company's profit formula *is* its business model. This is understandable since at the end of the day (or more precisely, the end of the fiscal year) every company hopes to have generated profit. But truly, it is only one element of the total business model.

KEY RESOURCES AND KEY PROCESSES

Key resources: The unique people, technology, products, facilities, equipment, funding, and brand required to deliver the value proposition to the customer.

Key processes: The means by which a company delivers on the customer value proposition in a sustainable, repeatable, scalable, and manageable way.

Although the delivery of a CVP usually requires a vast array of resources, just a few *key resources* spell the difference between success and failure. You need to ask, "What unique combination of personnel, technology, products, facilities, equipment, suppliers, distribution channels, funding, and brand are needed to support the customer value proposition within the constraints of the envisioned profit formula?" People are the critical resource to a

FIGURE 14

Key resources and processes

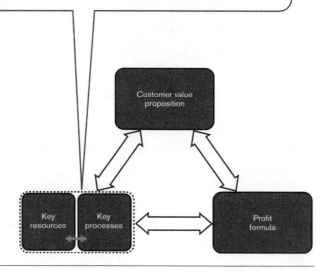

Key resources needed to deliver the CVP profitably. Might include:

- People
- Technology, products
- Equipment
- Information
- Channels
- Partnerships, alliances
- Funding
- Brand

Key processes, as well as business rules, behavioral norms, and success metrics that make the profitable delivery of the CVP repeatable and scalable. Might include:

- **Processes**: Design, product development, sourcing, manufacturing, marketing, hiring and training, IT
- **Business rules and success metrics**: Margin requirements for investment, credit terms, lead times, supplier terms
- **Behavioral norms**: Opportunity size needed for investment, approach to customers and channels

professional services firm. A consumer packaged-goods company might focus on its brand and channel retailers. As the world becomes more connected, companies no longer have to house all their own key resources; more and more look to partners to provide what they need. In *The World Is Flat*, Thomas Friedman describes Toshiba's innovative partnership with UPS. The shipping company furnishes not only transport but also electronics warranty, repair, and other critical back-end services, thus freeing Toshiba to focus on its core manufacturing expertise.[24]

Key processes are those recurrent, critical tasks that must be delivered in a consistent way, such as manufacturing, sales, service, training, development, budgeting, and planning. As with resources, the number of processes employed by a company may be vast. But the important ones to focus on are those that are crucial to serving the customer value proposition and profit formula. Although they are distinct elements of a successful business model and are the last to fully develop, I approach key resources and key processes in tandem. That's because the differentiation and sustainability of a successful business model depends on the unique way the key resources mesh with the key processes and how well they are knit together to repeatedly deliver the CVP and profit formula. In fact, the synergy between the key resources and key processes is as critical to the success of an enterprise as the key resources and processes are themselves.

Irish airline Ryanair's ability to provide a low-cost value proposition, for example, hinges on its related choices to service secondary airports, employ a nonunionized workforce, and ensure low overhead by, among other things, flying a standardized fleet of Boeing 737s and maintaining a spartan headquarters.[25] This potent combination of resources and processes work together harmoniously to support Ryanair's business model—a CVP of delivering radically discounted travel to customers through a profit formula reliant on high resource velocity and a low cost structure.

Before it began developing the Nano, Tata Motors followed a traditional automotive business model. It designed and built cars much the same way the industry had done since the Model T. But the key resources and key processes that made its truck and car lines so successful in India were of limited value to the Nano's new CVP and profit formula, with its lower unit margins, lower cost structure, and higher resource velocity. The challenge to create a car that was far less expensive than any model previously made forced Tata's Nano team to entirely rethink how it designed, manufactured, and distributed cars.

Tata began by deliberately searching outside the company to build a small team with fairly young engineers who, by virtue of their lack of experience, wouldn't feel constrained by traditional business models. This team designed a car that had dramatically fewer parts, producing significant cost savings and reducing the number of suppliers. Tata also reconsidered its vendor strategy: to reduce transaction costs and achieve better economies of scale, it outsourced a remarkable 90 percent of the Nano's components and used far fewer vendors than did the typical car in its fleet.[26] At the other end of the product cycle, Tata is considering a wholly new distribution strategy: shipping modular components of the Nano to a network of independent entrepreneurs who would then assemble them to order.

Whole Foods owes much of its success to key process innovations that organized what was an undeveloped and heterogeneous market. As noted earlier, Whole Foods originally relied heavily on supplies from small local producers—mostly organic farmers and makers of naturopathic products. In the 1980s, there was no national market for these products, nor any centralized distributors or product aggregators on which to build a large-scale national operation. To deliver its game-changing CVP, Whole Foods had to build a supply chain system unlike any that existed in the grocery business.

Whole Foods grew partly by regional acquisitions, subsuming the existing store brand, but since *local* was a key component of its CVP, the company let local store managers continue to make all purchasing decisions, effectively decentralizing its supply

FIGURE 15

The Tata Nano's business model

	Low-cost Indian car manufacturer	Tata Motors' Nano
Customer value proposition	Attractive, small automobile within my price range (Rs 2 lakhs, or US $4,000)	Get my family off the scooter for Rs1 lakh (or US $2,000)
Profit formula	High volumes at low margins; high margins in after-sales service; low direct costs	Higher volumes at razor thin margins; partially lower over-head costs; and radically reduced direct costs
Key resources and processes	• Low-cost production capabilities • Inexpensive parts sourcing • Cost-reduction strategies • Dispersed service network with skilled labor and capabilities for obtaining replacement parts and repair	• Patents on component inventions • Long-term, high-volume supplier contracts • Radically redesigned sourcing, manufacturing, and distribution processes

chain management.[27] As Whole Foods matured and its CVP became increasingly focused on high-quality perishables and pre-pared foods, it invested heavily in refining and systematizing this key process. It built discrete regional divisions and supplied them with its own national distribution network for specialty dry goods. To ensure high quality, it formed partnerships with local suppliers of organic perishables. Ultimately, it shifted most of the purchas-ing and distribution responsibility for private label and nonper-ishable items to its own warehousing and distribution operations, but it continued to let regional and local managers customize their product mix and stock directly from local producers.

Whole Foods innovated the traditional supermarket supply chain to serve its profit formula and achieved transformative growth in its white space. As a result, Whole Foods has grown from a single store staffed by nineteen people in 1980 to an effec-tive manager of about ten thousand suppliers, the bulk of them individuals or small, regional companies.[28] The decentralized nature

FIGURE 16

Whole Foods Market's business model

	Traditional mass market grocer	Whole Foods Market
Customer value proposition	Broad range of store brand, national, and premium-branded products; a time-efficient, self-serve experience	Convenient access to a broad range of foods and products that support environmentally and socially responsible practices; a pleasurable, high-touch shopping experience
Profit formula	Slim margins; emphasis on high-velocity dry goods and other items located in the center aisles	Higher margins; emphasis on produce, meats, prepared foods, and other fresh items located on the periphery
Key resources and processes	• Bargaining power with suppliers • Large-scale, centralized distribution network • Sourcing from national, regional, global networks • Standardized range of merchandise at all stores • Store designed to facilitate high volumes of purchases	• Relationships with local farmers and specialty merchants • Nine national distribution centers • Individual stores given autonomy to customize product mix, and stores individually organized from within • Stores designed to facilitate leisurely, social shopping experience

of the business model (and the key processes that fuel its success) enables individual stores to operate as if they were independent business units but still enjoy the benefits of being part of an extensive distribution network.

Whole Foods and the Tata Motors Nano demonstrate how incumbents can reinvent their business models to achieve transformational growth. These companies created integrated systems of key resources and processes that served important CVPs in powerful ways, driving their enterprises' success.

BUSINESS RULES, BEHAVIORAL NORMS, AND SUCCESS METRICS

Business rules, behavioral norms, and success metrics connect the elements of a business model and keep the system in proper balance. They ensure that the business can repeatedly and pre-dictably deliver the customer value proposition and fulfill the profit formula. Since their function is to perpetuate the existing operations, they tend to form last in the evolution of a business model. Over time, for example, Whole Foods overlaid rules and metrics on its decentralized management chain to make sure that its various regions adhered to the goals of its business model. Business rules and behavioral norms guided its distributed deci-sion-making network, and the company created a compensation system driven by team—not individual—metrics. Those controls helped Whole Foods Market achieve consistency in its day-to-day operations, leading to the greatest possible efficiencies and oper-ating profits.

FIGURE 17

Rules, norms, and metrics

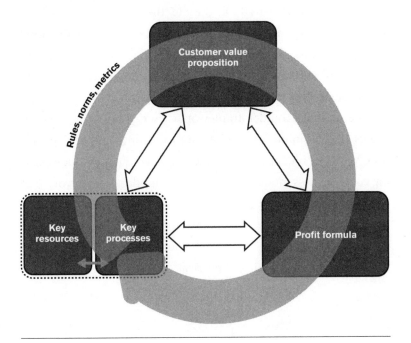

Eventually, the elements of the business model commonly fade into the mists of institutional memory, even as it lives on as a practical matter in the rules, cultural norms, and metrics. This may be the reason why so many companies can operate so effectively without being able to articulate what their business model is. But since they evolve precisely to optimize an existing business model, these guidelines and control mechanisms are powerful inhibitors to the introduction of new business models, an important paradox that will be explored more fully in chapter 8.

A SOLID BLUEPRINT FOR INNOVATION

A company venturing into its white space without a clear framework for business model innovation is like a contractor trying to build a house with no blueprint to guide him. He can generate a spreadsheet that tells him building a home would be profitable and then gather the resources needed to construct it, but when the lumber and concrete arrive at the site, the crew works aimlessly. Without a clear plan, any house that is built will probably look like the last house the crew worked on, because that's all they have to go on. If they do manage to create something original, it will have more to do with luck than with foresight.

The business model framework described in this chapter brings the discipline of architecture to business model innovation. With the blueprint it provides, you can diagram your existing core business model and design new models to help you seize your white space. The framework is the structure on which a manageable and more predictable innovation process can be built—a structure that can unlock your creativity as you pursue transformational growth and renewal.

Part Two

When New Business Models Are Needed

It is not the strongest of the species that survives, nor the most intelligent, but the one most responsive to change.

—Charles Darwin

Imagine you are a Formula One race car driver. You have been racing an extremely sophisticated, fine-tuned machine on the streets of Monaco for years. You've applied breakthrough innovations in engine and suspension technology, radical new tire designs, and myriad other improvements to make your vehicle the best, most cutting-edge platform possible. You continually work to refine your competitive strategy and on-course tactics for winning races, and you have consistently collected the checks and trophies that victory brings. You've built a successful and profitable team, and few competitors can keep pace.

One day, however, you look to new horizons to grow as a competitor. The Baja 500 catches your interest, a challenging off-road race that traverses the Mexican desert. So you head to Baja, California, and start adjusting your Formula One machine to the task of barreling over rocks, sand washes, dry lake beds, and mountain passes. You narrow the wheelbase, install knobby tires, retool the transmission, upgrade the springs and shocks, and enhance the engine to make it run better in 100-plus-degree heat. Once again, you study the course and develop a strategy. You're ready to compete when the starter flag falls.

You get dusted. No matter how many competitions you enter or how extensively you retool, your sophisticated Formula One machine simply cannot compete with rugged, kick-butt, off-road vehicles. All your experience, all your well-conceived strategies, and all your tactical prowess proves useless because your car is wrong for the Baja 500. If you want a shot at winning, you need a new racing platform.

So it is with white space and business models. To compete and win a different type of race—to profitably satisfy a new job with a new CVP in your white space—you need an entirely different business platform. You must reinvent your business model—changing all four elements and realigning the way they interact.

Not all new customer value propositions require business model innovation; businesses can create game-changing new CVPs in new markets (and sometimes new industries) by leveraging the strength of their core model. These are adjacency moves. P&G, for example, developed innovative products like the Swiffer disposable mop/duster and Febreze fabric and air freshener within the context of its existing business model. Swiffer turned the common household mop from a commodity into a branded, consumable product and transformed the market in the process. Febreze created a new market category—cleaners for fabric too large for the washer, like furniture and rugs—then extended into unique air fresheners. Both Swiffer and Febreze innovatively satisfied new jobs-to-be-done, but P&G produces and distributes them according to its existing homecare business model, which is optimized to manufacture and distribute consumable products in large scale.

How do you know if your new CVP requires a venture into your white space? You need a new model when, to fulfill the new customer value proposition, you find you must:

- Change your current profit formula, especially the overhead cost structure, the resource velocity, or both;

- Develop many new kinds of key resources and processes;

- Create fundamentally different core metrics, rules, and norms to run your business.

When one or more of these conditions is true, the new opportunity lies in your white space, and you will need a new business model to compete.

This section will help you gauge whether you can keep your Formula One race car or if you need to engineer a new dune buggy to tackle the next challenge The following chapters will identify a range of market circumstances that present opportunities or imperatives for venturing into your white space through business model innovation and describe how certain companies did it successfully. Chapter 3 examines how business model innovation can help you address your *white space within*—opportunities to fulfill important but unsatisfied jobs-to-be-done for your existing customers within existing markets. Chapter 4 describes how you can use business model innovation to create new markets in your *white space beyond*. Here, the focus is on democratizing products and services: that is, making them accessible to large groups of potential consumers who have been shut out of a market entirely because existing offerings are too expensive, too complicated, or too time-consuming. Finally, chapter 5 examines how the forces of industry transformation can create opportunities or imperatives that can be addressed through business model innovation in your *white space between*, the new terrain that emerges when some combination of transformative market shifts, innovative technology, or government policy creates massive industry upheaval.

The quest for transformative growth and renewal should be a proactive one, but the challenge in a new race is that you must first develop an eye for the most-promising opportunities. These chapters will help you see them in new ways.

The White Space Within

Transforming Existing Markets

*The real voyage of discovery consists not in seeking new
landscapes but in having new eyes.*

—Marcel Proust

D ow Corning began its corporate life as a joint venture
between The Dow Chemical Company and Corning
Glass Works to investigate and commercialize silicone technology.
In 1943, it launched its first product, an ignition-sealing silicone
compound that enabled high-altitude flight by inhibiting mois-
ture formation in aircraft engines.[1] Fueled by the aircraft needs of
World War II and the boom in commercial air flight that followed,
the company grew briskly and expanded into a wide variety of
industries, including construction, personal care, automotive, and
medical products. Through the years, Dow Corning's business
model powered a high-touch, solutions-oriented customer value

proposition with an impressive array of more than seventy-five hundred product SKUs.[2]

Then came disaster. In the 1990s, Dow Corning's silicone breast implants were alleged to cause various diseases, including breast cancer. Public outcry and massive class-action lawsuits led to a $3.2 billion settlement in 1998 that drove the company to seek bankruptcy protection.[3] By 2001, Dow Corning faced a critical juncture. As a capital-intensive business, it found itself with significant excess manufacturing capacity and stagnating growth in many key product areas.

To address these challenges, the company hired a new CEO, Gary Anderson, who quickly replaced most of the company's senior management and began a massive restructuring. Anderson then tapped a well-regarded Dow Corning executive, Don Sheets, to build a small team to examine the company's existing customers. By gaining a better understanding of the customer's unfulfilled jobs-to-be-done, Anderson believed, Dow Corning would uncover new opportunities.

Sheets' team soon realized that many of Dow Corning's customers were in a mature phase. They were experienced in silicone applications, had been using the company's products for years, and knew exactly what they wanted. The company's silicone had virtually become a commodity. "If you look at our customer surveys over the years," says Sheets, "Dow Corning's biggest concern was that our prices were too high. We were bundling our products and services together—R&D, product development, customer services—but a fairly large segment of customers just wanted to buy the product. They still wanted the same high-quality product and reliable supply, but they didn't want to pay for the services."[4]

With the Web boom still echoing, CEO Anderson suspected that there was an opportunity to create an Internet-enabled business to address this growing market. So he gave Sheets a big title, a million dollars, and one year to figure it out. Sheets understood that the real challenge was to stimulate demand at the low end of the market—despite the fact that every part of Dow Corning's existing business model and culture functioned to deliver solutions for the high end. "The task wasn't to sell on the Internet. I asked myself rather if there was a way to drive new demand into the company," Sheets says. "It quickly became pretty clear that to seize the opportunity, we would need a new business model."

Markets are born, grow, change, and die. Customer demand inevitably shifts, too, as do the jobs they need to get done. To stay relevant, you must remain vigilant to these changes and devise new ways to address them. In the early stages of market development, these new jobs can often be successfully addressed by sustaining innovations—new products, services, or features—that fit well within your existing business model. At later stages, these shifts are often more profound and require you to reconsider your business model or develop a new one. When that happens, as it did for Dow Corning, it brings the opportunity to *seize* your *white space within*: to achieve transformational growth or renewal within your existing market by delivering new customer value propositions, wrapped in appropriate business models, to address these new jobs.

THE SHIFTING BASIS OF COMPETITION

Opportunities in your white space within often relate to predictable shifts in an industry's *basis of competition*—the aspects of an offering for which a customer is willing to pay a premium price.[5] Each shift puts emphasis on a different kind of innovation. At the early stage of market development, companies typically compete for customers on the basis of *functionality*. During this stage, customers will pay more for product features, functions, and value-added services that more closely fulfill the practical aspects of their jobs-to-be-done. Companies tend to go after these essential jobs first, and they build business models ideally suited to delivering continual product innovation. They compete by improving their products and services while reducing costs and prices through greater efficiency.

When these offerings reach a good-enough level and performance-related jobs are mostly fulfilled, the basis of competition shifts. Customers will no longer pay a premium for additional performance improvements; they want *higher quality* and *reliability*. A product's functions and features become necessary but not sufficient to induce customers to buy. So companies must differentiate their offerings by better satisfying customers' desire for well-made and reliable solutions. At that point, process innovation becomes the key to success. Companies refine their existing model to improve processes like procurement, manufacturing, customer relationship management, and technical support services, placing a special emphasis on quality assurance and quality control.

When Japanese automakers entered the U.S. market in the 1960s, for example, they introduced small cars like the Toyota Corona to establish a foothold with price-sensitive buyers. In the late 1970s and early 1980s, however, they shifted the basis of competition by producing cars of significantly higher quality. Doing so didn't require a whole new business model; they made process improvements to key business functions like manufacturing and vendor management. Customers willingly paid more for high-quality, reliable cars, and that helped Japanese automakers move upmarket to serve the middle and high-end tiers of car consumers.

Once most of the functionality and reliability requirements of consumers are met, the basis of competition shifts yet again. Customers begin to demand innovations that allow them to fulfill their jobs-to-be-done more quickly, more easily, or in a way more precisely tailored to their individual needs. Companies now compete through *convenience* and *customization* to garner premium prices. Companies like Zipcar in North America and Britain and Daimler's Car2Go, recently launched in Germany, for instance, compete directly on convenience. Customers who want the convenience and freedom of a car but don't want to own one outright (perhaps to reduce their carbon footprint or simply to avoid the hassles of city parking) have happily signed on for these car-sharing services, which fulfill the job of a car without many of its drawbacks.

Finally, when a competitive offering accomplishes most jobs related to all three aspects of performance, the market becomes just about entirely commoditized. At that point, companies compete almost solely on cost. The progression is not always linear; the basis of competition can shift directly from reliability to cost. That often occurs in business-to-business companies and in

FIGURE 18

Shifts in the basis of competition

Companies compete on the basis of performance predominantly through product innovations. When the basis of competition moves to reliability, they tend to respond through process innovations. But once the basis shifts to convenience and cost, business model innovation often comes into play as well.

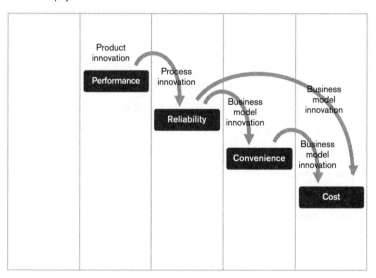

industries that are driven by technological advances like steel manufacturing and chemicals, as well as for OEMs like computer disk drive makers.

Whenever the basis of competition shifts to customization and convenience or fully to cost, customers' jobs-to-be-done change in fundamental ways (and so, therefore, does the needed CVP). So it is at these stages that companies most often find themselves at the limits of their current business models. To deliver value propositions that satisfy these new jobs and take advantage of the new opportunities for growth they represent, such companies must embark on business model innovation, as Dow Corning discovered.

DOW CORNING: THE ALCHEMY OF CHANGE

Many incumbents staring down the forces of full commoditization cede the low end of the market to competitors and chase higher margins at the top by clinging to their core business model. But that approach can seriously harm their long-term prospects. Dow Corning's Don Sheets thought there might be a better way. Focusing on customer jobs, he recognized that the company's market was shifting toward commoditization. If it wanted to grow, it might have to radically change the way it competed.

Sheets gathered his small team and began to formulate a customer value proposition that would fulfill the job-to-be-done of price-driven customers. The team targeted a price point 15 percent lower than current offerings.[6] This was an ambitious goal— not only because 15 percent represents a huge reduction in commodity pricing, but also because Dow Corning had a high-margin culture. Sheets knew that to build a business with any chance of success, his team would have to create a business model that could lower costs enough to deliver the kinds of margins that the company's finance people would accept.

Merely eliminating services would not do it. A 15 percent price reduction called for a profit formula that combined a dramatically lower cost structure with much higher resource velocity. So the team devised ways to remove inventory costs by limiting the range of allowable lead times and by manufacturing products only after an order was received. They increased velocity by selling and shipping in larger units, allowing far less variation in the size of orders, and eliminating value-added services, thus moving more silicone through the system faster. Breaking away from Dow Corning's traditional high-touch customized approach, the new venture needed to automate and standardize offerings to reduce overhead and the number of people involved in each transaction. That change called for a new key resource—a strong IT backbone that could automate the value chain and enable much of the business to be conducted online. This shift toward automation would have to be reflected in new business rules, which would need to be stricter than Dow Corning's old rules. For example, order sizes would be limited to a few, large-volume options; order lead times would be between two and four weeks; credit terms would be fixed; and rates for silicone would be set on the spot market rather than negotiated case by case. Customers that wanted exceptions to these rules would have to pay more.

As the vision for this new venture sharpened, the team realized how radical it was. The new business would be low-touch, self-service, and standardized—almost diametrically opposed to the model that governed Dow Corning's core operating space.

Seeing how different the new business would be, Sheets set out to determine if it could succeed within the confines of Dow Corning's core enterprise. He set up a war game to test the reactions of existing staff and systems to these strict new business rules. The new model got crushed. It was too foreign to Dow Corning's current modes of working. The way forward became clear. The new venture would need to be free from the core business model if it was going to thrive. To protect and nurture the opportunity, Dow Corning needed a new company with a unique identity. It launched Xiameter to seize its white space.

Following the explicit articulation of the new customer value proposition and profit formula, Xiameter focused on implementing and integrating the key resources and key processes it would need to succeed. Information technology, a small part of Dow Corning's core competencies, would be an essential piece of the new Internet-based business. So a small team quickly built a fully automated, Web-based order and delivery system. Xiameter's brand image also required careful attention: it needed to be connected to Dow Corning but be sufficiently separate for customers to understand that this was not their father's silicone company. Sheets settled on pairing a unique name, "Xiameter," with the tagline "The new measure of value. From Dow Corning" to emphasize both strengths.

Xiameter recognized that its people would be a key resource, but the need for low overhead kept staff size small. Some employees would have to act decisively in a fast-changing market, a behavioral norm not critical to Dow's core operations. "Xiameter was going to be about making fast decisions," says Sheets. "Most of the organization was going to be traders on the front lines, making decisions about where to set prices according to the spot market, and there were going to be big implications for those decisions. I needed people who could make good decisions quickly—those who would thrive in a fast-changing environment filled with a lot of ambiguity."

To import expertise from the parent company without importing the mind-set of the core, Sheets searched to identify Dow Corning staffers who, while they were team players, didn't quite fit into its culture. "We were looking for expert people who really knew their markets," says Sheets, but also were "the willing-to-stick-their-neck-out people." During interviews, when Sheets found likely candidates, he asked them to take the new job on the

FIGURE 19

Dow Corning and Xiameter

	Dow Corning	Xiameter
Customer value proposition	Customized solutions, negotiated contracts	No frills, bulk prices, sold through the Internet
Profit formula	Negotiated prices, high overhead, high margin	Spot-market pricing, low overhead, lower margins, high throughput
Key resources and processes	• R&D • Sales • Service orientation	• IT system • Lowest-cost processes • Maximum automation

spot. That allowed him to gauge how comfortable they were with making quick decisions. "This was exactly the right attitude I was looking for," says Sheets. "A different caliber of people than the traditional Dow Corning salesperson, for sure."

Having articulated a clear CVP, constructed an appropriate profit formula, and put the key resources and processes in place, Xiameter needed institutional patience and protection to allow it to find its way. Dow Corning, for its part, wanted to control development costs and make sure reasonable accountability metrics were put in place. So Xiameter developed an aggressive timetable for launch but deliberately kept the scale of the operation small so that team members could learn as they went. "Milestones were critical," says Sheets. "We set deadlines and worked feverishly toward them. This fast-paced environment allowed us to show early results while simultaneously developing a unique mini-culture within Xiameter."

As Xiameter took off, it began to deliver unexpected benefits to Dow Corning as a whole. Xiameter's lower prices enabled Dow Corning to utilize its substantial excess manufacturing capacity profitably. Over time, new customers helped fill industry capacity, driving up prices overall and increasing profitability in the core. Because Xiameter's model allowed it to capitalize on opportunities in times of market instability—changing its prices every hour if it chose to—it could respond to fluctuations in raw material and energy costs much more rapidly than Dow Corning could, which also raised profits.

Xiameter paid back Dow Corning's investment in just three months and went on to become a major, transformative success. Before it launched Xiameter, Dow Corning had no online sales component. Now 30 percent of sales originate online—nearly three times the industry average.[7] Although Xiameter began with existing customers, most are now new to the company, those who couldn't previously afford Dow Corning products. According to Sheets, "When Xiameter started pouring orders into our manufacturing facilities, people woke up. This was not just some Web thing; this was affecting real people, real manufacturing operations, real profits. And that was awesome."

As Dow Corning learned, in crossing the competitive threshold to a fully commoditized state, many times you need to reexamine your business model. To go from the high end and compete at the low end, a company must typically redefine its profit formula, key resources, and key processes to lower costs through greater automation, and this often means stricter business rules that reduce variability and standardize offerings.

Dow Corning recognized the shift in the job-to-be-done of some of its existing customers early, before it could be disrupted by competitors or new entrants. By embracing business model innovation and building a model ideally suited to serving these new jobs, Dow Corning seized its white space and created a powerful new engine of transformational growth.

COMPETING ON CONVENIENCE

Competing head-on with a new customer value proposition targeted at the low end of the market is one response to commoditization. Sometimes companies can sidestep the rush to the bottom altogether and instead shift the basis of competition from reliability to convenience and customization. Doing so often requires them to stop concentrating solely on product or process innovations and consider more multifaceted ways to deliver value. Product manufacturers, for instance, may need to add an educational component to a previously successful product or adopt a more flexible manufacturing process to meet the needs of increasingly demanding customers.

In the early days of the PC industry, for example, companies like Apple, Compaq, IBM, and Tandy addressed functional jobs in the market, and their innovations focused on product improvements. Apple became an early leader because its well-integrated products satisfied the performance needs of the market better than competitors' offerings. Its products were more reliable (they crashed far less often) and were much easier to use. Other companies played catch-up, innovating both products and processes to deliver better performing and more reliable computers. Then Dell Computer changed everything.

Dell computers were not initially as good as those of the established PC manufacturers, but Dell wasn't competing on the features and functionality of its products, which were already good enough in the eyes of most consumers. Instead it introduced a new level of customization and convenience to the PC industry. Dell's unique business model allowed customers to pick up the phone (and later, log on to a Web site) and order exactly the computer they wanted, preloaded with exactly the software they needed, delivered to their door almost overnight. This new business model—from its offering (customized product, direct sales, and forty-eight-hour delivery) to the way its products were sourced and assembled (just-in-time supply chain)—was nothing like the way personal computers had been made and sold. As a new entrant into the PC market, Dell forcibly shifted the market from competing on product features and reliability to competing on convenience and customization.

Twenty years later, the PC market is nearing total commoditization. The technological innovation curve for personal computing devices has moved so far beyond good enough that almost any product, sold in just about any way, is more than powerful enough for most users and can be conveniently obtained through many retail channels. Prices and margins are dropping fast. Now the question is whether Dell, once the innovator, can reinvent its business model to address a new CVP. For the next new industry, the time to full commoditization might be even shorter.

In fact, to a large degree, developed markets now exist in what might be called the *Convenience Era*. New product innovations aimed at functionality and quality jobs do not sustain themselves as long as they once did. The push for more convenient offerings comes ever more quickly. More entrants compete on this basis sooner and, as a result, markets move to total commoditization more quickly than they did in the past. Dow Corning's silicone business and Dell's PC business took decades to shift toward full commoditization; for newer industries, the time frame is shrinking.

Still, the Convenience Era brings not only threats but opportunities. Liechtenstein-based toolmaker Hilti, faced with the maturation of its power tool market, learned that sometimes they are indistinguishable.

HILTI: DRILLING DOWN ON BUSINESS MODEL INNOVATION

Compared with the extremely large and complex machinery produced by firms like Caterpillar, the handheld power tools Hilti makes are simple and inexpensive. While large equipment costs can run into the millions of dollars, a reasonably sized construction site would typically contain only about $20,000 worth of Hilti's products. In each small tool, however, lies great opportunity cost: a malfunctioning or broken item can halt construction for a day or more, costing exorbitant sums in lost productivity and delayed time lines.

In the late 1990s Hilti realized that its market was commoditizing and many of its product technologies were overshooting customer expectations. Further incremental improvements would not maintain market share or drive growth. "We found ourselves losing ground to competitors in the small-tool market," says Marco Meyrat, executive board member and head of worldwide sales and marketing. "We are a premium brand, and in that segment premium was of less value. Differentiation was harder for us to attain."[8] But Hilti wasn't prepared to cede the market, so, like Dow Corning, it turned to its customers to determine its next move.

During this process, Hilti identified a side effect of power tool commoditization: construction workers viewed these tools as virtually disposable. They often left them in the rain, maintained them poorly, or forgot them at the site. Neglect decreased productivity and increased repair costs for companies already struggling with thinning margins. At the same time, the profusion of cheap battery-powered hand tools left worksite tool tables scattered with mismatched components from different manufacturers. Maintaining and transporting tools was burdensome to customers, and it was becoming a growing challenge for construction sites to manage their "fleet" of tools over the course of a project. "Tool management is a pain," says Hilti's chairman and former CEO, Pius Baschera. "A construction crew's purpose is to build a house, not manage tools."[9] Predicting which tools, and how many of each, would be needed on a given day was complex. For big customers, process costs were becoming even more of a headache than repair costs; the added hassle of trying to organize and account for tools taxed already-strained resources. In short, though hand tools themselves were commoditizing, managing them had become difficult, and that represented a higher cost.

By examining the new job-to-be-done of its customers, Hilti saw that commoditization—its dreaded enemy—had actually created the opportunity to change the game in the power tool industry by competing on convenience and customization. Recognizing the way its customers were using (and abusing) its products, Meyrat and his team conceived of a leasing model for fleets of tools. Instead of buying power tools individually and dealing with their upkeep and management on their own, customers could pay a monthly fee to have a full complement of tools at their fingertips, kept well inventoried and in full repair. "The value proposition for the customer was basically, 'We take care of everything, and he always has the newest technology and the safest tools, well organized and readily available,'" says Meyrat.

Though the new business seemed logical and built on what looked at first blush to be Hilti's core expertise, this leasing model represented a fundamentally new customer value proposition, and Hilti's profit formula would have to adjust accordingly. "Clearly, it was a complete change in how we looked at revenue. The customer no longer pays up front by buying the tool. He gets and uses the tool, and we get the money month by month," says Meyrat. What's more, Hilti could no longer move inventory off its balance sheet every month; it would have to become a service business, both leasing tangible assets and providing new forms of intangible services. Sales transactions would be fewer in number but much larger in size. Margins would be higher, but so would overhead and administrative costs. In short, to meet the unserved jobs of its customers, Hilti would have to venture far from the safe confines of its core manufacturing and sales business to compete in its white space within.

Because this new CVP had come directly from its existing customers and many of the tool-related elements of the model were familiar, Hilti was able to quickly design a rudimentary blueprint for its offering and profit formula. Then it began to work out the key resources and key processes it would need. Contract management was its first priority. Customers would want the flexibility to add or remove individual tools from their contracts at any time. Because the new CVP was all about reducing customers' administrative costs, Hilti would have to maintain these complex contracts itself, an intense backroom capability that it would have to build from the ground up. To be profitable, Hilti would need to keep these costs low and be very disciplined with its customers about contractual add-ons. Additionally, the company had to devise a process to manage and maintain fleets of tools more inexpensively and effectively than its customers had. And it required a constant supply of fresh tools that could immediately replace ones that broke.

On the customer management side, Hilti needed to develop a Web site that would allow construction managers to view all the tools in their fleets (or several fleets at different sites) to monitor their usage rates. This data would help managers conveniently handle the cost accounting associated with these assets.

Meyrat says, however, that the greatest key-resource challenge Hilti faced was training its sales force to do a thoroughly new task. Fleet management is not a half-hour sale; it takes days, weeks, even months of meetings to convince customers to change their behavior and buy a program instead of a product. "This was not spot selling, which is what we mostly did, but rather going into partnership with customers over a number of years," he explains. Suddenly, field reps accustomed to dealing with crew leaders and purchasing managers in mobile trailers on site found themselves sitting across a conference table from CEOs and CFOs, since typically only an executive can sign off on such a program. They needed to wear suits, not work clothes. "Our salespeople confessed that they didn't have the courage to go up to the C-suite," says Meyrat. So Hilti committed significant resources to overcoming these cultural barriers.

To test its assumptions and develop the model, Hilti kept the initiative small at first, establishing a foothold market to prove—and improve—the proposition and thoroughly work out all the new key resources and processes the business model required. "We started in Switzerland, which we consider a home country, where we have strong brand position, deep customer relationships, a high-quality customer base, and a stable currency," explains Meyrat. Hilti began the new business with just eight customers, and the results were immediately encouraging. "When I looked at the share of wallet we were getting and their behavior, I saw they were not only giving us their tools but a larger share of their consumables budget," recalls Meyrat. "When I started to extrapolate the numbers for these few customers, they were almost magiç in terms of what was possible."

Seeing profit early, Hilti could afford to be patient for growth as it continued to develop the right combination of contract management and accounting rules and metrics to allow the business to scale up. Initially, for instance, Hilti stipulated that it would

FIGURE 20

The Hilti business model

	Traditional power-tool company	Tool fleet management services
Customer value proposition	Industrial and professional power tools and accessories	Comprehensive tool fleet management service to increase on-site productivity
Profit formula	Low margins, high inventory turnover	Higher margins; asset-heavy (tool leasing); monthly payments for tool maintenance, repair, and replacement
Key resources and processes	• Distribution channel • Low-cost manufacturing plants in developing countries • R&D	• Strong direct sales approach • Contract management • IT systems for inventory management and repair • Warehousing

present this option only to large customers. But it quickly learned that small and medium-sized construction firms that used as few as fifty Hilti tools also found the proposition attractive, albeit for different reasons. To them, unexpected costs of repair and replacement had a big impact on the bottom line, and scaling up for peak loads presented a serious financial challenge. The new offering enabled these smaller customers not only to hedge against the downsides but also to scale more nimbly and efficiently in upturns.

Hilti piloted the program in 2000, and within three years rolled it out throughout most of the worldwide markets in which it operated. The program has grown steadily, enrolling thousands of companies around the world and accounting for a significant part of Hilti's tools and overall sales revenue.

FULFILLING UNSERVED JOBS IN EXISTING MARKETS

Shifts in the basis of competition may create an imperative to venture into your white space within through business model innovation. But opportunities can arise whenever customers have jobs-to-be-done that are not fulfilled by existing CVPs. FedEx, for example, used a jobs-based focus to introduce a new business model to the package-delivery industry even though the industry was not in the process of shifting.

As an undergraduate at Yale, founder Fred Smith flew charter planes out of Tweed New Haven airport to make some extra money. At the small northeastern airports he frequented, he noticed that many of the corporate jets belonging to the rising powerhouses of the electronic age, companies like IBM and Xerox, were being used to transport high-priced components to field service engineers who were repairing computers. People needed these expensive parts, and they needed them right away; speed was clearly more important than cost. One company—Emery Air

Freight—was trying to address this job, but it had built its infrastructure around passenger airlines serving large cities. At that time, the aviation industry was heavily regulated, and airlines flew mostly point-to-point routes, so reaching smaller cities was difficult. Emery was "force-fitting the rapid movement of high-value-added and high-technology products into a transportation system that wasn't designed for it," explains Smith.[10]

Seeing an opportunity, Smith envisioned a fundamentally different business model uniquely designed to serve a single unaddressed job-to-be-done: reliably move valuable packages from point A to point B overnight. He bought a small aviation company and, to fulfill that job, created an integrated air and land system based on a then-revolutionary hub-and-spoke approach. It blew Emery out of the market. Beginning in 1971 from a humble fleet of fourteen small aircraft serving twenty-five U.S. cities, Federal Express became in 1983 the first U.S. company ever to book $1 billion in revenue without a merger or an acquisition.[11]

High-end overnight delivery remained a niche market until government deregulation of air freight opened it to letter and document transport. Vast numbers of consumers wanted to send documents and other packages reliably from city to city overnight, and they, too, were willing to pay a premium to do it. FedEx's business model was uniquely suited to satisfy that need. The U.S. Postal Service and UPS had held government-protected near-monopolies in this market, and neither was prepared to respond to the new entrant. (Although overnight package delivery might seem to be a natural extension of UPS's core efforts, the company's business model focused on ground transportation, relied on existing air routes and carriers, and couldn't initially deliver the speed or reliability the market wanted.) It took UPS and the U.S. Postal Service years to transform their business models to catch up.

Furniture maker IKEA is another example of a newcomer that transformed an existing market. It integrated a unique business model to address the job-to-be-done of young couples who want low-cost but fashion-forward furniture. The idea is transformative because it's not merely about lowering the cost of furniture (which many discount houses already were doing). What IKEA did was turn furniture from a durable into a nondurable good. High-quality, big-ticket furniture is an investment. It's a high-stakes purchase because people have to keep it for a long time to get their investment back. Buying IKEA's furniture is more akin to buying clothing—something its young customers could do over and over again, as they moved from apartment to starter house to larger house, or just grew out of their adolescent taste. That's why the furniture needed to be both radically less expensive than the high-end alternatives but also far more trendy than the discount offerings.

To further cement the value proposition, IKEA combined the shopping experience of a showroom with the convenience of a logistics facility: after seeing the furniture in hip, stylish rooms, customers buy their selections in modular and easily transportable kits, which they can take home the same day and assemble themselves. All the products and services (in-store childcare, heavily discounted food) are backed up by a profit formula and key resources and processes uniquely integrated to deliver its CVP.

Similarly, as we saw in the previous chapter, Whole Foods Market built an integrated business model that satisfied the unserved jobs of its high-end customers. In all three cases—FedEx, IKEA, and Whole Foods—incumbents were slow to recognize and largely unable to respond to the unique nature of these new business models, which were aimed squarely at their white space within. It can be argued that it's easier for start-ups to capitalize on such opportunities, since incumbents are hampered by the imperatives of their existing business models, a problem start-ups simply don't have. But that needn't be the case: whether newly emerged from shifts in the basis of competition or lurking unrecognized within a market, unserved jobs-to-be-done in an existing industry present powerful opportunities for transformational growth and renewal for incumbents as well, through business model innovation.

4

The White Space Beyond

Creating New Markets

*One does not discover new lands without consenting
to lose sight of the shore for a very long time.*

—André Gide

ndia is home to 16 percent of the world's population—
but to 28 percent of the world's hair.[1] This is a very
good statistic if you happen to sell shampoo, and it's one of the
reasons why Hindustan Unilever has nearly tripled its sales and
profits over the last five years.[2] The company has for years been a
market leader in personal care products, initially finding success
among India's rising middle class and then introducing a wide
range of brands appealing to low-income market segments. Leadership in such a rapidly developing market might seem to guaran-
tee a long run of growth. But by the end of the twentieth century,
thanks to shrinking profit margins and increased competition,

Hindustan Unilever needed to find new markets and new growth, according to newly installed CEO Nitin Paranjpe.

That would not be easy. The world's second-most-populous country had an average annual income of just $600, and large swaths of its inhabitants lived in poverty. But Hindustan Unilever's leadership was determined, and in 1999, the company formed a task force of middle managers, Paranjpe then among them. "We were charged with finding new ideas and new models to help the organization," he says.[3]

Meanwhile, dramatic changes were afoot in Indian society. The once tightly controlled economy was liberalizing quickly, and the government had begun a wide-scale effort to improve the quality of life in rural India. "India lives in its villages," the saying goes. In fact, 72 percent of India's 1.13 billion people live in the countryside.[4] Most of the 600,000-plus villages are remote, and their roads can't handle large shipments of goods or much commerce above a subsistence economy. Rather than invest in expensive infrastructure, India's government chose to support the creation of self-help groups composed predominantly of women. The idea was to assist rural entrepreneurs to start businesses and so improve living conditions in their regions.

Hindustan Unilever recognized in this changing social dynamic a new customer opportunity and was determined to be one of the first companies to capitalize on it. "Rural India was approaching an inflection point," says Paranjpe. "The challenge was to turn it into an opportunity."[5]

DEMOCRATIZING PRODUCTS AND SERVICES

While business model innovation provides you with a powerful process to exploit your white space within existing markets, it is equally effective in unlocking even more exciting opportunities to serve entirely new customers and create new markets—to seize your *white space beyond*. Seizing your white space beyond means developing new business models in support of customer value propositions aimed at potential customers who are currently *nonconsumers*. Nonconsumption occurs when large groups of potential customers are shut out of a market because existing offerings are too expensive or complicated for them or they lack access.

To open up new markets and address their jobs, a company must first determine what factors prevent those jobs from being met and, more fundamentally, what barriers constrain consumption by the underserved customers. When customer value propositions can be developed to break through those barriers to consumption, new markets open up for the company as its solutions become available to nonconsumers, effectively *democratizing* products and services.

There are four main barriers to consumption: wealth, skills, access, and time.[6] Tata's Nano helps scooter families break through the *wealth barrier* that prevented them from owning a safer, more comfortable means of transportation. Software maker Intuit devised the accounting software QuickBooks to fulfill the job of many small-business owners, "Help me not run out of cash," and broke the *skills barrier* that excluded them from more sophisticated and complicated offerings like Peachtree. Whole Foods Market helped relatively wealthy consumers break the *access barrier* by organizing the chaotic natural foods and organic produce markets into one rational, locally available supply chain. And Minnesota-based MinuteClinic (now owned by CVS) broke the *time barrier* to health care by putting nurse practitioners in drugstore kiosks and offering treatment for simple medical ailments without appointments and within about thirty minutes.

Nonconsumers fall all along the socioeconomic spectrum, although opportunities to democratize products in emerging markets and reach the so-called bottom of the pyramid are particularly ripe. The global economy daily creates new opportunities for innovative companies to bring goods and services to those previously unable to access them. As the global economy fuels upward mobility for even the poorest in developing nations, many companies are finding growth by breaking down barriers for consumers they previously thought to be unreachable, unprofitable, or both.

For example, the infrastructure costs involved in delivering telecommunications services to remote rural areas once made such services unfeasible in developing countries. Now cellular technology—distributed through a leasing model by companies like América Móvil and Vodafone—has changed that dynamic. In the 1990s, Chinese appliance maker Galanz gained a foothold in the world microwave-oven market by building small, energy-efficient models that could be used in cramped Chinese apartments whose power supplies were limited. With a business model that was profitable at domestic Chinese price points, Galanz opened up a vast market of nonconsumers and went on to capture nearly 40 percent of the world market.[7] The South African Bank Absa created an innovative franchise model for a profitable microlending division that promoted economic development in townships while also recruiting nonconsumers into the financial services sector.

"We're living in an era where the technologies that have empowered high living standards and 80-year life expectancies in the rich world are now for almost everybody," notes economist Jeffrey Sachs, director of Columbia University's Earth Institute. "Not only do we have a very large amount of economic activity right now, but we have pent-up potential for vast increases [in economic activity] as well."[8] Recognizing this enormous potential in the remote villages of rural India, Hindustan Unilever acted to seize its white space.

HINDUSTAN UNILEVER: THE SHAKTI INITIATIVE

When Hindustan Unilever started its search for new opportunities, it set up a task force with a clear mission: devise a model that could break the wealth and access barriers that kept hundreds of millions of nonconsumers from the market. And do so in a way that would improve lives—do well by doing good, as the company came to think of it. Task force members found inspiration in the microfinance model of Grameen Bank started by Muhammad Yunus in Bangladesh and began to envision a business model centered on partnerships with the government-supported and microcredit-financed village self-help groups. This venture, called the Shakti Initiative, would reach out to these embryonic entrepreneurs, identifying and training a sales force termed the "Shakti Ammas" (literally *strength mothers*). These women—who had little or no business skills—would act as direct representatives for Hindustan Unilever in their villages. For the company, it was a radical idea on many levels. "First, we had to break the mind-set that said it was not viable to go directly to a village with two thousand people in it," says Govind Rajan, now Hindustan Unilever's general manager and category head of skin care. "Then we realized that we could give something back to society on a large scale in a mutually beneficial manner."[9]

To build a partner network, Hindustan Unilever needed to reconceive its approach to distribution. "We always saw distribution as something *we* did," says Rajan. "We never thought about a direct-to-consumer approach. We went in, serviced the dealers, and got out. As we went along with Shakti, we learned about connecting and partnering. This was the first time we ventured into managing businesses at a micro scale."[10]

To work closely with rural self-help groups, microcredit lenders, nongovernmental organizations (NGOs), and the Indian government—the forces that were changing the nature of the market—required new skills and new processes. "It is an entirely different mind-set to work with people who are not P&L-oriented," says Rajan. "Their passion is for society and how people feel about themselves."[11]

The team knew it needed to build an appropriate platform, so it worked hard to clearly define the target customer. Ultimately, members arrived at a surprising customer value proposition: Shakti was not really about delivering products to the end user; it was about delivering a business opportunity. The Shakti Ammas were the true new customer. "Delivering a business opportunity became the white space play," says Paranjpe. "We focused on the channel, delivering adequate training and support to ensure their profitability. We would only succeed if every member of the channel succeeded as well."[12] By defining the direct representative as the customer and focusing the value proposition on giving her a viable business opportunity, Hindustan Unilever built a model designed for long-term growth that was difficult for competitors to replicate. Though rival Nirma, an Indian consumer- and industrial-products company, had beaten Hindustan Unilever to the direct sales approach, Hindustan Unilever hoped its unique focus on a partner network model would give it an infrastructure and expertise that differentiated the company in the rural market.

Early on, Shakti team members realized that the profit formula for this new model would have to tolerate low margins as the offerings gained a foothold in communities unaccustomed to purchasing branded products.[13] They expected these margins to be balanced by increased volume, and they also included the social benefit of the enterprise in their metrics for success, a position supported by Hindustan Unilever's corporate leadership. To test the assumptions underlying the Shakti model, Hindustan Unilever started in only one region. Just seventeen women began selling hand soap, shampoo, and a small list of other products in their village market and then went increasingly door to door.[14]

Since the customer value proposition was to serve the channel, Shakti needed to provide sales training and business support for the Ammas—new key resources—to help them understand the brand and to run a profitable small business.

"This was not a typical customer development project that could be executed through traditional MBA skills," says Krishnendu Dasgupta, the channel manager who has been part of the Shakti team since 2005. "We needed new skills and a different mind-set."[15] These women had varying levels of education, so Hindustan Unilever couldn't simply hand them routine training manuals. Instead, the Shakti team created training audio cassettes and invited the women to attend classroom programs in the nearest locations.[16] Because advertising and marketing were also unfamiliar concepts, in some cases the Shakti team hired troupes of local actors to travel from village to village performing comedic skits—a live commercial extolling brand messages.[17]

Many of those messages focused on the benefits of increased hygiene. Teaching a rural population the benefits of washing hands before eating—thus decreasing intestinal infections, a leading cause of childhood mortality—made the Ammas more than Avon ladies; it gave them increased social stature because they provided an important benefit to the village.

"We wanted to improve the quality of life, but it also had to be profitable," says Sanjiv Kakkar, now the chairman of Unilever Russia, Ukraine, and Belarus.[18] The team's efforts paid off right from the start. The average Shakti entrepreneur brought in enough money to effectively double her household income, and the impact on the community was palpable. "Every time I visited a Shakti family I could see the happiness in their faces. Shakti changes lives. People have touched my feet, an honor normally reserved for elders only," says Dasgupta.[19]

But challenges remained. Getting product to remote villages required further innovation in distribution. Many of the target markets lacked paved roads. At first, Shakti leveraged Hindustan Unilever's existing rural distribution network, arranging drop-off points for the Ammas to pick up their weekly deliveries, which they often would transport to their villages on carts towed by bicycles. As it incubated the model, however, the team found that it was more efficient to develop entrepreneurs in geographic clusters. By reducing the number of drop-off points, local distributors made higher profits, and Shakti could decrease stock requirements, which in turn increased efficiency and resource velocity.[20]

As the Shakti team honed the profit formula and refined the key resources and processes to nail the job-to-be-done, operations expanded to sixty women by the beginning of 2003 and then to twenty-eight hundred women entrepreneurs covering twelve thousand villages by the end of that year.[21] To protect growth, the core team stayed focused on its CVP of delivering a powerful business opportunity. "Our metrics were all about establishing viability," says Paranjpe, "not sales volume. We wanted to put as little pressure on the distribution stream as possible until we proved its viability." Accordingly, the Shakti team rigorously analyzed all the elements of its business model, carefully considering the cost of reach, watching for possible cannibalization of Hindustan Unilever's existing rural streams, and adjusting the model at every step. "Only when we understood how the model could work did we start to scale up," says Paranjpe.[22]

The Shakti Initiative lost money for the first three years, during the investment phase, as the model was established. Extrapolating from the early profitability of the Shakti Ammas' efforts, however, the team clearly saw that overall profit would soon follow scale. "This kept us from being overanxious for growth," says Paranjpe.[23]

By 2007, the model had been refined and tested extensively: It was time to ramp up the business. Shakti expanded to forty-five thousand Shakti Ammas covering more than one hundred thousand

FIGURE 21

Hindustan Unilever and the Shakti Initiative

	Traditional consumer packaged goods business	Hindustan Unilever Shakti Initiative
Customer value proposition	Retailer is the customer. Distributes product through established third parties in concentrated population centers	Shakti Amma woman is the customer. Deliver not just a product but a business opportunity to Shakti Amma women, who represent and sell HUL products in their villages. "Do good while making a profit"
Profit formula	Low per-unit cost; economies of scale; large inventory	Initially lower margins but much greater quantity; high trade margins on low-per-unit-cost products
Key resources and processes	Distribution as an internally focused process	Distribution through • Partner network • Training and distribution systems • Creative direct marketing • New brand message (focused on health)

villages across 15 states in the country, and reaching over 3 million homes.[24] For their villages, the Shakti Ammas bought the equivalent of almost $100 million worth of consumer goods from Hindustan Unilever in 2008.[25]

Thus Shakti became an engine of transformational growth for Hindustan Unilever, dramatically increasing its rural penetration and adding new perspectives, capabilities, and expertise to the parent company. "Shakti occupies a very special place in my heart," concludes Dasgupta. "I wake up every morning and go to work at Hindustan Unilever knowing that I am contributing to society and improving the lives of thousands of underprivileged people. It makes me very proud."[26] Shakti's partner network model is now a platform for Hindustan Unilever's next stage of growth. Furthermore, the company believes it can replicate the model in many parts of the developing world, democratizing offerings for millions more nonconsumers and unlocking vast new markets.

DEMOCRATIZING KNOWLEDGE AND UNDERSTANDING

Chapter 3 discussed how shifts in the basis of competition can create opportunities within your market. A similar phenomenon can open up new markets. Like the bases of competition, the way we solve problems also shifts over time, depending on how much we know about them. When we know very little, we tend to guess a lot, and when we know a lot, we tend to follow well-known patterns or specific rules to find solutions. This is what's known as the *problem-solving continuum*. As the problem-solving ability within an industry progresses along this spectrum, opportunities in your white space open up, allowing you to develop new customer value propositions and new business models that democratize products and services and overcome barriers to consumption.[27]

To illustrate how knowledge shifts along the problem-solving continuum and see the opportunities that result, let's look at the challenge of determining if a woman is pregnant. Before the advent of modern medicine, people simply guessed, stumbling around in the metaphorical dark for some clear indicator that a baby was on its way. The ancient Egyptians wet bags of wheat and barley with the urine of a possibly pregnant woman; if the grain germinated, they believed the woman was pregnant. Hippocrates suggested that a woman drink honey water at bedtime; if she suffered abdominal distention and cramps, he postulated she was pregnant. Through the nineteenth century, the most reliable method was the careful observation of a woman's own physical symptoms, such as morning sickness or the fact that she missed her menstrual period for several months.[28]

Around 1927, however, doctors discovered that when they injected the urine of a pregnant woman into a female rabbit, it often (but not always) produced bulging masses on the rabbit's ovaries called *corpora hemorrhagica*. A knowledge pattern had emerged, the first shift on the continuum. Unfortunately, the only way to see the ovaries was to kill the rabbit (so every rabbit died, even if the woman wasn't pregnant). It was an expensive and complicated procedure, but the pattern of information it revealed produced more certain results. Then medical science advanced further. We learned that a hormone called human chorionic gonadotropin (hCG) caused the ovarian bulges, and researchers developed a blood test to detect its presence.[29] Knowledge shifted again to deliver a rule-based solution to the problem; a certain level of hCG definitely meant pregnancy.

Thus as medical knowledge grew, the way we attacked the problem shifted along the problem-solving continuum from unstructured problem solving (crude visual and tactile examinations) to pattern recognition (the rabbit test) to rule-based decision making (blood test). Interestingly, once this knowledge became rule-based, a business model innovation occurred in the medical industry. Blood tests were relatively expensive and required highly skilled technicians to perform them accurately, so many women were nonconsumers. In the wake of the discovery of hCG, in 1977 Warner-Chilcott introduced e.p.t., the first home pregnancy test, which broke both the access and skills barriers to predicting pregnancy.[30] By moving a medical diagnostic procedure from the doctor's office to the home, this offering democratized critical information, allowing almost anyone to get it.

Certain archetypal business models lend themselves well to problems that lie at different points on the problem-solving continuum.[31] Unstructured problem solving and early pattern-recognition approaches are best delivered by a business model archetype called *solution shops*.[32] These comprise professional service companies like doctors' offices, law practices, accounting firms, consultancies. They provide customized solutions to unique problems, and their primary resources are people and knowledge. Since neither the outcome itself nor the time invested to produce one can be clearly predicted, businesses of this type usually bill in

FIGURE 22

Business model archetypes

	Solution shop	Value-adding process business	Facilitated network
Customer value proposition	Experts draw on intuition and problem-solving skills to analyze problems and then recommend solutions	Provide scaled products and services to fulfill more pattern-recognition and rule-based jobs-to-be-done at lower cost	Connect users with similar jobs-to-be-done into a system where they can exchange, share, buy, and sell goods and knowledge with other participants
Profit formula	Fee for service, high margin, high overhead, low resource velocity	Fee for outcome, lower margins, low overhead, high resource velocity, scale	Membership subscription, advertising, and transaction-based fees
Key resources and processes	People and knowledge	Predictable processes, integrated systems, manufacturing	Size and composition of customer base; IT system that enables connectivity
Examples	System integrators, law firms, consulting firms, advertising agencies	Retail, manufacturing, education, food services	Consumer banking, online auctions, Internet bulletin boards, telecommunications

units of time for services rendered. They tend to be high-margin, high-overhead, low resource-velocity operations.

As knowledge progresses to clear pattern recognition and rule-based decision making, *value-adding process businesses* produce high-volume solutions at a lower cost.[34] These are integrated-product companies; their success lies in their ability to invent, manufacture, market, and distribute their goods or services at scale. Given the increased predictability, such firms can make their money on actual output (the product or service rendered). These businesses tend to have lower margins and lower overhead than solution shops; they also have higher resource velocity and are more dependent on size and on achieving target profitability through scale. Their ability to scale is what allows them to democratize knowledge and, ultimately, provide greater access to products and services. Most manufacturing operations fall into this category, and so do such services as MinuteClinic, the pharmacy-based medical kiosks mentioned above.

MinuteClinic recognized that although medical knowledge had changed dramatically since the middle of the twentieth century, the model by which medical care is practiced had not. Doctors practice in solution shops—service businesses where difficult problems such as diagnosing Parkinson's disease are addressed alongside simple, well-understood procedures like detecting strep throat. The doctors bring high-level training and associated expense to every diagnostic procedure, whether it requires these skills or not. MinuteClinic recognized that advances in medical knowledge had pushed ever larger amounts of basic medical treatment down the problem-solving continuum into the realms of clear pattern recognition and rule-based care, where less well-trained, and therefore less expensive, nurse practitioners could adequately perform the work.

MinuteClinic took advantage of a shift in the basis of medical knowledge to disaggregate simple rule-based diagnostic procedures from complex, unstructured ones. The innovative business model it wrapped around this customer value proposition broke barriers to consumption of basic medical care. Since 2000, MinuteClinic's decentralized, pharmacy-based kiosks have allowed people to walk in without an appointment and be treated by a nurse practitioner capable of diagnosing a limited number of common low-level ailments using rule-based diagnostics.[34] While still playing out, MinuteClinic's model is a legitimate attempt to democratize basic health care by introducing a value-adding process business into an industry long dominated by solution shops.

A third business model archetype, *facilitated networks*, provides the backbone systems with which like-minded customers can exchange goods and services, share information, collaborate, or socialize with little intermediation. Two long-standing examples of these include telecommunications networks and financial exchanges like the New York Stock Exchange (NYSE). Many more of these kinds of businesses have emerged with the advent of the Internet, which through its capacity to connect individuals to one another and to vast amounts of information further democratizes knowledge. Online brokerage businesses like eBay and Craigslist and many of the innovative Web 2.0 businesses like Facebook, Twitter, Yelp, and LinkedIn are based on this model, which usually makes money through transaction fees, advertising, or subscriptions that trade on levels of participation in the network.

Facilitated networks democratize knowledge not only by making it more accessible but also by connecting individuals who have incomplete but complementary knowledge. Together, they can dramatically enhance the problem-solving process, shifting knowledge to pattern recognition and rule-based decision making more quickly and in a cost-effective manner. Think of the open source movement, where software developers collaborate to improve the Linux computer operating system. Think, too, of the many medical Web sites dedicated to sharing information about various chronic diseases. The Restless Legs Syndrome (RLS) Foundation's site, for example, is explicitly intended to push knowledge about the condition along through a grassroots effort. It describes itself as a place where patients can "arm themselves with information to educate health care providers about RLS."[35]

Every day, advances in technology and knowledge, combined with increased access to more information, create opportunities to reach nonconsumers and open new markets. But as we've seen with the examples in this chapter, to democratize offerings with new customer value propositions frequently requires specialized resources and processes and a different profit formula. Failure to consider how all the elements of the business model work together can doom a new initiative trying to democratize its offering.

In 1997, for example, SAP and Intel launched Pandesic, a joint venture to bring a simpler, less-expensive version of SAP's enterprise resource planning software to small and medium-sized enterprises (SMEs).[36] SAP historically targeted huge corporations, but that market was becoming saturated. The SME space has always been something like the promised land—vast, disorganized, and filled largely with nonconsumers of comprehensive ERP solutions. But the qualities that make it a tempting market also make it a tough nut to crack. Smaller businesses rarely have the resources to buy customized enterprise solutions, the skills to learn how to use them, or the IT departments to maintain them. They are constrained from consumption by wealth, time, and access barriers. The market needs solutions that can break down these barriers, and Pandesic was an attempt to seize this market in SAP's white space.

Being the offspring of two tech companies, Pandesic treated the challenge as a technical, product problem. It was led by managers who were deeply familiar with huge, complex global organizations, established markets, and well-defined product lines but had utterly no experience identifying and establishing an initial foothold in a new market with a disruptive product. Perhaps not surprisingly, then, its offering quickly evolved into a complex, automated end-to-end solution, which was neither easy to learn nor easy to operate. It marketed the product through the same channel partners that sold SAP's large company systems—IT implementation consultants such as Accenture. That core sales channel, however, had few incentives to sell Pandesic's simpler product, which didn't need implementation support, when it could make substantial money on traditional SAP products. Encumbered by the business model that worked so successfully in SAP's core markets, and not fully realizing that reaching this new customer required a different business model, Pandesic failed miserably. It shut its doors in February 2001 after having burned through more than $100 million.[37] SAP failed to develop a unique business model to reach its white space. MinuteClinic and Hindustan

Unilever, by contrast, realized that in order to deliver solutions that break barriers to consumption and democratize markets, they needed new business systems. MinuteClinic's opportunity arose when the basis of medical knowledge shifted. Hindustan Unilever seized its opportunity when the jobs-to-be-done of a large group of nonconsumers at the bottom of the pyramid became easier to address, in part because of external government policy changes. That's one of the tectonic shifts that form the subject of chapter 5.

The White Space Between

Dealing with Industry Discontinuity

Economic progress, in capitalist society,
means turmoil.

—Joseph A. Schumpeter

In the early nineteenth century, most people lit their homes with lamps that burned whale oil. In midcentury, as supplies were constricting and prices rising steeply, Canadian physician and geologist Abraham Gesner developed kerosene, a cleaner-burning alternative made from a plentiful resource—crude oil—and founded what became the modern petroleum industry. Whaling, a major world industry, virtually ceased. Then Edison threw a light switch, and the world changed again. No one wanted the foul smell and dangerous flame of kerosene lanterns in their homes when they could have clean and easy electric light. Demand for fossil fuels plummeted.

The advent of the automobile jump-started the fossil fuel industry again. Plentiful and cheap carbon-based fuels went on to transform the way we live on the planet—how we travel, heat our homes, and build our cities. The oil industry flourished, the chemical industry evolved on its back, and automobile manufacturers emerged among the titans of the Manufacturing Age. Today, the ramifications of climate change threaten the automobile, utilities, and oil industries. The world seems to be on the cusp of a new energy paradigm, one with the potential to radically alter any number of industries as businesses struggle to adapt.

Chapters 3 and 4 focused on innovating business models primarily in response to market-driven circumstances. Those shifts tend to emerge from identifiable and predictable trends that alter industry structures and redraw industry lines over time. But there clearly exist less predictable, more revolutionary forces whose roots often lie outside the market—the attacks of 9/11; the commercialization of Internet technology; the global push to address greenhouse gas emissions; Deng Xiaoping proclaiming, "To be rich is glorious" and unleashing the Chinese commercial dragon; the financial meltdown in the fall of 2008—that can alter the course for everyone in the race. These acute, episodic events can come with little warning (like a tsunami) or with leading indicators (like a cyclone), but they share two characteristics: First, they dramatically change the game, prompting the need for new customer value propositions and new business models for entire industries and sometimes whole economies. Second, their ramifications are extraordinarily difficult to predict. But like the shifts already discussed, tectonic industry change—when whole industries suffer an unforeseen shock, collapse, or form anew—opens up uncharted territory for companies between what was and what is to be, in the *white space between*.

Myriad forces can contribute to tectonic industry change, and they can vary radically from one shock to the next. For the purpose of our discussion, I will focus on three that directly create opportunities or imperatives for business model innovation:

- Unpredictable or radical shifts in market demand (sweeping changes that go beyond the sort of predictable evolution of markets I've already described)

- Discontinuous shifts in technology (that is, the development of revolutionary enabling technologies)

- Dramatic shifts in government policy targeted at the business environment

Each of these forces can bring about sudden changes on their own, but they often work in concert to produce even more volatile discontinuities, each influencing and amplifying the effects of the others.

When faced with industry discontinuity, many companies falter. Some fail to recognize the complicated external forces propelling the event, or if they do they're unable to trace the implications correctly or completely. Others hold tightly to their old paradigms and try to adapt them gradually to meet the changed circumstances. Adaptation in the face of dislocation can help a company ride out the storm, but business model innovation can bring about *renewal* by creating a new business platform uniquely suited to the radically altered terrain.

TRANSFORMATIVE MARKET SHIFTS

A business must always be sensitive to changing market conditions, of course, but occasionally market demand shifts unexpectedly and far more fundamentally than can be reasonably predicted, certainly much more abruptly than the evolutionary shifts discussed in the last two chapters.

You might think the defense industry would have a lot of experience with cataclysmic events, and so it does. But that has not always translated into change in its business model. During the Cold War, the U.S. military valued large-scale, expensive, and complex weaponry that could deter an opponent with the threat of widespread destruction. Consequently, the U.S. military procurement process evolved to manage large-scale, expensive, and complex projects, and defense contractors logically built complementary business models: solution shops that specialized in relatively high-margin, low-volume offerings. When the Cold War ended, the industry evolved, to some degree. Throughout the 1990s, military operations were downsized, but the era of big, bloated project development and procurement continued.

Then came the attacks of 9/11 and the subsequent wars in Afghanistan and Iraq. The nature of combat shifted dramatically, and with it, the marketplace of war. Suddenly, the military, the defense procurement system, and the contractors that served it had to change their ways of working. A centralized, command-and-control mind-set had to yield to decentralization if soldiers were to get the information and versatile weaponry they needed.

The soldier's job-to-be-done when faced with a diffuse enemy in the towns of Afghanistan and Iraq is radically different from what it was in the Cold War. Soldiers need mobile body armor, better-protected vehicles, and ubiquitous two-way communications, as well as troop-level surveillance and reconnaissance devices—not more advanced battleships and fighter aircraft. Delivering solutions for the new job-to-be-done of equipping a mobile, fast, decentralized military will require the armed forces to adopt a new business model, one capable of developing and procuring good-enough solutions for the soldier in volume and in a manner more responsive to rapidly changing conditions on the ground. Consequently, the prime contractors and other providers of equipment and technology for the defense industry will need to shift more of their businesses from solution shops to value-adding process firms with new business models capable of quickly and economically producing this equipment en masse. But they must also retain a part of their business as traditional solution shops to continue to equip the armed forces with large-scale weapons systems.

Another tectonic shift in market demand, which has yet to fully play out, began when China and India opened their economies and brought billions of potential nonconsumers into the global market. The advent of microlending further fueled this explosive shift in demand, putting capital and disposable income into the hands of potential rural consumers and aspiring small-business owners and creating opportunities to fulfill a host of jobs-to-be-done for these erstwhile nonconsumers.

If these opportunities weren't tempting enough, there are the related effects of the global financial contraction of 2008 to consider as well, which substantially shrank consumer demand in Western markets. They may remain constricted for some time. As demand shifts from West to East, Western multinationals looking for growth must enter these developing markets with new insight and creativity and not expect that all they need to do is tweak their current business models to account for local differences. In that regard, they might take a look at the innovative models that some emerging-market multinationals are using to great effect. China's Goodbaby, for example, has mastered the trick of offering a vast selection of baby carriages, high chairs, playpens, and the like at the low end by making up for slim profit margins through the high volume that even niche markets in China can command. And already some emerging global companies are applying that and other lessons creatively to Western markets—Chinese appliance manufacturer Haier set up a kiosk in New York's Times Square one hot summer's day and sold seven thousand air-conditioners in seven hours.[1] In any event, no global company, wherever it's based, has the luxury of ignoring this tectonic shift.

TECHNOLOGICALLY DRIVEN SHIFTS

As my colleague Clayton Christensen first recognized, new technologies are not inherently disruptive; whether they are or not depends on how the technology fits with each company's existing business model.[2] Newly discovered enabling technologies can in fact sustain and expand existing markets, strengthening industry incumbents and their current models. The Internet, for example, made it easier for Charles Schwab to deliver its no-frills, do-it-yourself discount brokerage service to customers who wanted to manage their own investments. It similarly enabled Dell Computer to be even more effective at selling its personal computers directly to consumers. And it enhanced the existing mail-order pharmacy business model for Medco, greatly facilitating its fulfillment of pharmaceuticals to millions of customers every month.

And, as we saw earlier, technologies can help companies transform existing markets or create new ones. In chapter 3, we saw how the Internet enabled Dow Corning to create Xiameter's low-touch, low-cost customer value proposition, transforming its existing market by seizing its white space within. And this book started with the story of how hybrid airship technology presented Lockheed Martin with an opportunity to create a new market by going into its white space beyond.

But, of course, the technology that serves as one company's opportunity is often another company's—and often an entire industry's—disruption. In the 1960s, for instance, electric arc furnace technology made it possible to produce steel at significantly lower cost than the large integrated mills of Big Steel companies could. Firms like Nucor and Chaparral Steel wrapped innovative business models around this mini-mill technology and began to pick off customers from Big Steel for such low-end products as construction rebar. In this classic example of Christensen's disruptive innovation concept, mini-mill technology gradually improved, and those companies moved upmarket, nearly wiping out Big Steel and transforming the entire industry.[3]

Similarly, in the late 1990s, MP3 compression technology made possible the MP3 player. Apple ultimately responded to the new technology with its innovative iPod/iTunes business model in 2003, cutting the bottom out from under compact disc manufacturing and disrupting the Sony Walkman and its prevailing music-retailing business model in the process. That same technology—variously evolved to MP4 and other digital-compression technologies— now threatens entertainment broadcast models as well. *Enabling technologies* such as these are powerful forces because they can influence and disrupt a number of industries simultaneously— and create opportunities for companies in their resulting white space. Waves of enabling technologies over the last two centuries have spawned new industries that require new business models and have often made obsolete the earlier technologies and associated business models.

Arguably the most potent of these technologies since the light bulb is the Internet. While, as I've said, it clearly holds the potential to sustain a company's current business model both within and beyond its current markets, the Internet's greatest effect has certainly been on the creation of new business models that have transformed industries. More than 30 percent of the roughly 350 business model innovations that my colleagues and I have studied over the past ten years have been enabled by Internet technology.[4] In fact, the very idea of business models gained prominence with the Internet boom of the late 1990s. Think of eBay's auction business model, which hinges on facilitated networks made possible by Internet technology. Or Amazon's online retail business, or

FIGURE 23

The industries and infrastructures of each technological revolution

Technological revolution	New technologies and new or redefined industries	New or redefined infrastructures
First From 1771 *The Industrial Revolution*	• Mechanized cotton industry • Wrought iron • Machinery	• Canals and waterways • Turnpike roads • Water power
Second From 1829 *Age of steam and railways*	• Steam engines and machinery • Iron and coal mining • Railway construction • Rolling stock production • Steam power for many industries	• Railways • Universal postal service • Telegraph • Ports, depots, and worldwide sailing ships • City gas
Third From 1875 *Age of steel, electricity, and heavy engineering*	• Cheap steel • Full development of steam engine for steel ships • Heavy chemistry and civil engineering • Electrical equipment industry • Copper and cables • Canned and bottled food • Paper and packaging	• Worldwide shipping in rapid steel steamships • Transcontinental railways • Great bridges and tunnels • Worldwide telegraph • Telephone • Electrical networks
Fourth From 1908 *Age of oil, the automobile, and mass production*	• Mass-produced automobiles • Cheap oil and oil fuels • Petrochemicals • Internal combustion engines • Home electrical appliances • Refrigerated and frozen foods	• Networks of roads, highways, ports, and airports • Networks of oil wells • Universal electricity • Worldwide analog telecommunications
Fifth From 1971 *Age of information and telecom-munications*	• Cheap microelectronics • Computers, software • Telecommunications • Control instruments • Computer-aided biotechnology and new materials	• World digital telecommunications • Internet, e-mail, and other e-services • Electricity networks • High-speed physical transport links
Sixth From 2003 *Age of cleantech and biotech*	• Renewable energy led by solar, wind, and biofuels • Energy efficiency • Energy storage technologies • Electric vehicles • Nano materials • Synthetic biology	• Enhanced electricity transmission capabilities • Decentralization of power generation • Connection of electricity and trans-portation energy infrastructures • Increased availability of water and electricity • Extensive gene data bank links

Source: Carlota Perez, *Technological Revolutions and Financial Capital: The Dynamics of Bubbles and Golden Ages* (Northampton, MA: Edward Elgar Publishing, 2003), 14.

Google's creation of the search market with its advertising-based business model.

Just as certainly, new Internet-driven business models have brought many old-guard industries to their knees. It's easy to think of examples. There's the *Encyclopaedia Britannica*, whose customer value proposition was dramatically disrupted over a decade ago by the good-enough Encarta, and then further undermined by the not-good-enough Wikipedia combined with the incalculable resources of Google's search engine. Then there's the travel agency industry, disrupted by online competitors like Expedia and Travelocity, aggregators like Kayak and Travelzoo, and advice sites like TripAdvisor. Perhaps the most talked-about and widespread disruption is the one going on right now in the newspaper industry. Newspapers' problems can be (and have been) framed in myriad ways, but a couple of points stand out when we take a look at their plight through the business model framework.

Practically from the start, newspaper companies saw the Internet as a threat and framed it as such. But they failed to see in it an opportunity for growth: They devised no new customer value propositions. They conceived of no new revenue models (or other ways to change their profit formula). Instead, they merely took the look and feel of the newspaper and put it online, stretching thin the resources and processes of their existing model. Newspapers held on to their value-adding process–type business model, pumping out its product in volume to a mass market, even as their readership gravitated toward more customized offerings.

In the meantime, the Internet-based competition of Google News, Drudge Report, and Huffington Post have segmented and democratized news content. Sites like Craigslist and Recycler have endowed the classifieds job with greater reach. And user-based review sites like Yelp and Chowhound have undermined news organizations' former advantage in local food and entertainment expertise. In picking off readers, they have picked off advertising dollars as well. Each of these new companies has leveraged the Internet in a facilitated network model to capture consumers and make money in a fundamentally different way. Looked at through the business model lens, the problem newspapers need to address is how they, too, can leverage the Internet to serve their customers' need for greater customization and use their incumbent content generation and editorial-filtering strengths to address head on their new, disruptive competition.

SHIFTS IN GOVERNMENT POLICY AND REGULATION

Though the social contract that binds consumers and markets together within national boundaries often evolves slowly, dramatic or sudden shifts precipitated by acute political or social forces on the world stage do occur, even in relatively stable developed nations. Shifts in public opinion, consequent realignments in political leadership, the emergence of new national priorities, or sudden changes in the availability or cost of key resources can result in fundamental shifts in the nature of markets, the jobs-to-be-done within those markets, and the business models that will allow companies to thrive in the new environment.

For instance, in 1973, deregulation of the health care industry in the United States gave rise to health maintenance organizations (HMOs), preferred provider organizations, and a wide range of other new intermediary models. Similarly, deregulation of the European airline industry in the 1990s broke the stranglehold enjoyed by the national carriers and created opportunities for low-cost entrants like EasyJet and Ryanair. These upstarts tailored their business models to compete on price, which democratized air travel. That policy shift, by extension, altered the landscape of tourism and economic development throughout the Continent, as hundreds of thousands of people who once could not afford airfare suddenly started traveling—and to once-out-of-the-way cities served by the low-fare carriers.

Public investment in a new social priority can also alter the course of private industry. After India's economic liberalization began in 1991, the tightly controlled corporate environment exploded, allowing new entrants to thrive throughout the nation. A later decision to focus government efforts on village-level economic development and government support of microlending cooperatives created the opportunity for Hindustan Unilever to build its business model innovation with the Shakti Initiative. Understanding powerful external forces according to how they change the jobs-to-be-done in the marketplace and create opportunities for new models can make the sometimes overwhelming far more manageable. Instead of hunkering down and waiting out the storm, or freezing your current model like a deer in the headlights, you can transform and renew your company by building business models that take unique advantage of the shifting environments. Let's see how that might work to address the seemingly intractable problem of climate change.

BETTER PLACE: THE MAKING OF AN ELECTRIC VEHICLE MARKET

The global shift away from fossil fuels and toward clean and renewable energy will affect almost every industry and every consumer worldwide, changing consumption habits, manufacturing and distribution systems, financial models—indeed, the very way everyone on the planet lives. Changes in market demand, technological advances, and government policy are converging on this most pressing of global issues. Perhaps few transitions could be more complicated. Consumers in industrialized nations will not accept greener solutions that surrender the efficiencies and convenience that the carbon-based economy has provided them. Those in developing countries mostly lack the resources to adopt green technologies on a scale large enough to make any real difference to the environment. Technologically, the spotlight has focused on a succession of alternatives for power generation—wind, biomass, solar, geothermal, fuel cells—but it's unlikely that the need for green energy will be satisfied by any single alternative alone.

It will probably take a combination of technologies introduced in stages. Around the world, governments and policy experts are considering green energy initiatives and legislation, but they have yet to reach a clear consensus on which solutions to support. Because solving the clean energy challenge will necessarily involve large investments in public and private infrastructure and massive upheavals in mature industries, active government involvement and clear policy direction is crucial. But what has been missing in the current conversation is a comprehensive business model innovation that takes into account all three sets of forces—technology, policy, and market.

One company that has started down this path is Better Place. Founded by Israeli entrepreneur Shai Agassi, its approach to the challenge of creating a mass market for electric cars represents a radically new business model geared to seizing an entire industry's white space. Its success is by no means assured, but as a pioneer, its progress is well worth examining.

Better Place began with a simple but monumental question: How do you run a country without oil? The answer seems simple, too: electric cars have been around almost since the dawn of the automobile industry. But no one has figured out how to generate the economies of scale needed to produce them at a profit. How, then, do you go about effecting a wholesale uptake of clean, efficient electric cars?

The search for an answer has always focused on the technology. The key resource that's held automakers back is the battery. Current battery technology is expensive and can't store enough energy to power a car as far as drivers want to go without recharging. Reliable and mass-producible batteries exist, but the best of them run only about one hundred miles and take several hours to recharge.[5] For these and perhaps other reasons, most automakers have made very limited investments in developing and commercializing electric cars.

Shai Agassi didn't limit his focus to technology. He began by examining the jobs-to-be-done of the automobile consumer. What he discovered didn't make his task any easier. First, he realized that most consumers don't want to share a car. Cars mean independence and flexibility. Few people want to give that up in the name of conservation, as numerous failed attempts to encourage carpooling clearly show. Drivers also want cars that are big enough to hold five people. They want their cars to handle responsively and be fun to drive (few people are content to putter around in two-seat electric golf carts). Consumers also want their vehicles to be affordable to buy, own, and operate, and—as a social job-to-be-done—acceptable to be seen in. Finally, they don't want to have to stop to refuel more than about fifty times a year, for more than five minutes at a time.[6]

Interestingly, Agassi's analysis revealed that consumers do not view the cost of ownership in the aggregate; they focus more on the costs of purchase and maintenance. While some consider fuel economy to be a critical feature, most don't place a car's ongoing energy costs high on the list of factors that determine their purchase decision; they are by and large willing to pay whatever gas costs to own a car that meets their acquisition budget and social requirements. Most won't pay, say, $10,000 more for an electric vehicle of equivalent performance to a gasoline vehicle, even if it costs dramatically less to run.[7]

Agassi also saw that there was something of a social contract underlying the way people use gas-powered automobiles. Car-dependent societies promise their citizens the ability to travel freely, to live where they want, and to commute to work and recreation.[8] Most urban infrastructure is designed to accommodate these needs, with good roads and convenient opportunities to refuel and repair. At heart, then, the gasoline economy is enabled by a well-entrenched and extensive infrastructure that makes gas-powered autos a convenient and affordable solution to consumers' various jobs-to-be-done. To construct a viable electric offering, Better Place would have to make electrons just as convenient and affordable.

Digging deeper, Agassi's analysis revealed that cars fulfill two distinct jobs. Most people live in *transportation islands*—the space they drive in every day, which extends on average only twenty miles or so. Fulfilling that job is well within the capacity of existing battery technology. But periodically, people take longer trips, and it's for this job that electric vehicles fall short. Since most drivers can afford only one car (or would not buy a special-purpose short-haul car), common sense dictates that to make Agassi's vision of a gasoline-free society work, one car must do both jobs. The industry was stuck on how to solve for range extension.

With this analysis, Agassi thought he had his customer nailed. He knew the job-to-be-done of a new car buyer; he just had to figure out how to serve it. But then he met former U.S. president Bill Clinton, who helped Agassi realize that he was concentrating on the wrong part of the car market. Only 50 million new cars are purchased each year. Far bigger is the market of nonconsumers of new cars: some 700 million people buy used cars every year. If you focused only on new cars, you could perhaps build a company that could sell twenty thousand vehicles, but that wouldn't make the world a better place. What if, Clinton suggested, you could give these people an electric vehicle for free? That would essentially put the resale value of a new gasoline-powered car at zero. "Clinton helped me see that if you get the used market to switch over to an electric vehicle," Agassi says, "it would force the new car market to totally flip-flop overnight, because no one would finance new gasoline-powered cars anymore."[9] The world would tip to cleaner cars almost immediately.

Pondering this seemingly insurmountable challenge—to give away electric cars for free—led Agassi to his big insight. What could make it worth a company's while to give away a car? The same thing that makes it profitable for a company to give away a razor—the blades. Agassi realized that what he needed to focus on was not selling cars, but selling the underlying job cars did—moving people over many miles—and that was a job traditionally done by gasoline. "The way users consume miles today is in the form of a car," says Agassi. "I had to figure out a way to replace the oil-fueled miles they consume with electron-fueled ones."[10]

What if, Agassi thought, we divorce ownership of the car from ownership of the battery? Instead of thinking of the battery as a durable part of the automobile, what if it was considered part of the energy infrastructure? A new CVP began to take shape: a radical improvement on the gasoline-based infrastructure that was his true competition—more convenient, less expensive, and easier to use.

To solve the convenience problem, Better Place would build infrastructure in advance of an actual electric car market, developing a massive network of charge spots to hook up the last foot of the electric grid to the last foot of the parking infrastructure. Charging locations would be linked by GPS to powerful back-end computer networks, so drivers would know where to park, and when they returned, their cars would be fully charged. To solve the problem of extended range, Better Place would build battery-switching stations that operated much like car washes. Travelers would drive their cars in, the depleted battery would be removed, and a fully charged one installed—in less time than it took to fill a gas tank. The batteries then could be charged at night, when electricity costs are substantially lower.[11]

This CVP would satisfy consumers' jobs-to-be-done, but what sort of profit formula could make it work? Agassi crunched the numbers. Electricity is much cheaper per mile than gasoline. Electric-car batteries today cost about $10,000 (if you don't have to honor a warranty or add a profit margin), and they get about two thousand charge cycles, each one allowing the car to go roughly one hundred miles. That translates into a cost of about 5 cents per mile.[12] A kilowatt hour of cleanly generated electricity costs about 10 cents in volume and gets four to five miles, or 2 cents per mile, so the total cost of energy for an electric vehicle is about 7 cents per mile (at the time of this writing). There have been few breakthroughs in improving battery capacity but many promising developments in battery life. The technology currently being tested promises to almost double the number of charge cycles by 2015, effectively halving the cost, perhaps, to as low as 3.5 cents per mile. With the price of gasoline in the United States averaging 10 to 15 cents per mile and prices in Europe as much as triple that, selling miles that cost only 3.5 cents seemed like a good place to begin.[13]

In the end, Agassi did not think up a way to give electric cars away for free anytime soon (at least not until electricity costs go down even further and gasoline prices increase even more). But a viable model came into focus. Better Place would adopt a facilitated network business model, providing the infrastructure and services that enabled electric cars to satisfy the needs of the market.

Much like a cellular communications company, Better Place would use the margin between what electricity costs and what people paid per mile for gas to subsidize the cost of new electric cars. In fact, it could sell electric miles the same way a consumer buys cellular minutes, with multiple subscription plans designed to appeal to different driving segments; heavy commuters, city drivers, and so on.

So far, this model involves only business forces and technological developments. But as radical as those are, Agassi knew his model would also need the backing and the intervention of the government. No public infrastructure on the scale necessary to support a new transportation paradigm could succeed otherwise. Too much of the existing infrastructure and economy—from auto dealers to banks to oil companies—would be disrupted. The costs of implementing such a massive infrastructure, even in the smallest foothold market, would be too large and too risky to undertake unless the market grew far faster than it would if left to its own devices. Government could provide incentives to jumpstart the transition. In this respect, active government involvement is a key resource for delivering Better Place's CVP.

Agassi realized Israel could be an ideal foothold market. It is relatively small geographically (few people drive more than twenty miles at any one time), and cars seldom leave the country. "It is a perfect transportation island," Agassi likes to joke. "If your car is leaving the country it's been stolen."[14] In 2006, Agassi approached Israel's then–vice prime minister, Shimon Peres, with his idea and won a champion. Peres encouraged Agassi to go ahead with his plan, having recently crafted legislation to support electric vehicle adoption. Under its terms, buyers of gas-powered cars would pay a 72 percent tax on their purchase, whereas buyers of electric vehicles would pay only 10 percent, thus speeding the shift to an all-electric fleet.[15] This measure would give Better Place the rapid market uptake required to make its model viable.[16] With the network model and a willing government sponsor in place, Better Place needed to secure two more key resources: automakers and funding. With Peres's support once again, Better Place won agreement from the Renault-Nissan alliance to mass-produce electric vehicles and the batteries needed to run them. With the tax break, the cars cost about half what an average sedan in Israel currently does.[17]

FIGURE 24

Business model innovation at Better Place

	Traditional car sales	Better Place
Customer value proposition	Convenient and affordable transportation. Buy or lease vehicle	Convenient and affordable transportation. Buy or lease vehicle; but have access to a recharge network, which includes the batteries through a mileage plan
Profit formula	Charge for the vehicle; high margins on service and resale	Charge for access to recharge network—similar to wireless carrier model, except customers pay for miles instead of minutes; low margins on the car
Key resources and processes	• Management of a large inventory and in-stock parts • Consumer financing • Ancillary businesses (rental cars, body shops, corporate sales, etc.)	• Network of strategically placed charging stations to recharge vehicles after short trips • Network of battery-switching stations to recharge vehicles on long trips • Software to tell vehicle where it can charge and when

Interestingly, Better Place is now conducting a similar effort in Denmark, and things are moving rapidly. The Danish government is planning to impose a 180 percent tax on gas-powered cars but none at all for electric vehicles. That Better Place is pursuing its model in both countries at once, though, raises the question of whether the risk would be better managed if it proceeded sequentially so that it could apply what it learned in one place to the next.

Better Place's model is, to put it mildly, a massive undertaking—to fundamentally alter the way customers consume personal transportation. Will it work? It's too early to say. It's easy to be skeptical but far more valuable to follow the progress of this ambitious project for what it can teach us about the possibilities of wholesale infrastructure transformation in the white space between.

Part Three

Business Model Innovation as a Repeatable Process

*Innovation is risky but it's not random. Innovators
have a disciplined invention process. They may not be able
to articulate it, and sometimes the Eureka! moment happens
in the shower, but it stems from a disciplined process.*

—A.G. Lafley

This book began with a framework to define a business model, one that illuminates the underlying value-creation engine of any business. Part II examined various situations that are particularly ripe for business model innovation, in existing markets, in creating new markets, and in confronting industrywide upheaval. Part III now turns to the "how," shifting from a predominantly descriptive approach to more of a prescriptive one.

The companies discussed in the previous section that successfully seized their white space have many traits in common. They all had bold and courageous leaders with open minds and an intuitive sense for where transformational growth could be found. These leaders all had a willingness to reconsider the structure of their existing business models in the pursuit of new customer value propositions. They all had imagination, skill, and a bit of luck. What they largely lacked, however, was a systematic approach to business model innovation.

From their experiences, and those of a number of other companies I've worked with and studied with my colleagues at Innosight and elsewhere, I have extracted patterns and principles, and designed a structured approach to business model innovation. Instead of relying on intuition and luck to unlock transformational growth, you can follow a business model design and implementation process that brings predictability to seizing your white space.

The process consists of three basic steps, the first of which does not involve thinking about business models at all. It starts instead with the opportunity to satisfy a real customer who needs an important job done. The clearer your understanding of the job-to-be-done, the more powerful and enduring the customer value proposition you can develop. The second step is to construct a blueprint that lays out how your company aims to fulfill that job at a profit. This is where the business model framework presented in chapter 2 comes in. In conceiving of and comparing this blueprint with your existing model, you will determine if fundamental business model change is necessary. The third step is implementation—working out in practice how the physical key resources and processes must come together to deliver in reality on the abstract concepts of the CVP and the profit formula. During this step you'll also decide whether this new business system can be managed in an existing business unit or if a new business unit needs to be created for it to flourish.

The job is rarely understood clearly at the outset, and the details of the blueprint won't nearly be fleshed out during its initial conception, so managers must understand the work of business model design and implementation as a process of testing hypotheses and applying lessons learned rather than one of rigid execution.

Chapter 6, then, examines in detail the first two steps in the business model innovation process, from identifying a job-to-be-done to creating a powerful customer value proposition to drafting a blueprint of your new business model and comparing it with your existing model. Chapter 7, which focuses on implementation, reveals how to bring your model to life while maximizing your chance of white-space success. Taken together, these two chapters present a fresh approach to developing and scaling a new business, a method useful for start-ups and incumbents alike. Chapter 8 explores the unique and complex management challenges that incumbents face while building new business models or reinventing their existing one.

6

Designing a New Business Model

First comes thought; then organization of that thought, into ideas and plans; then transformation of those plans into reality. The beginning, as you will observe, is in your imagination.

—Napoleon Hill

Ratan Tata looks out over a road in New Delhi and conceives of a car that can compete with scooters. Marco Meyrat comes up with a brilliant plan to transform Hilti's tools from a commoditizing product into a high-end service. Hindustan Unilever creates thousands of new hair-care customers by radically reconceiving the nature of distribution. Dow Corning's Don Sheets envisions a new way to capture the low end of the silicone market. All of these inspiring stories can be downright depressing. No one wants to depend on something as fickle as inspiration to create a new business.

No one should have to. Conceiving of a truly innovative new business model does not need to be purely (or even mostly) a matter of imagination, inspiration, serendipity, or luck. It can be an orderly process that, like Stanislavsky's acting exercise, uses structure to unlock creativity, rather than the other way around.

At its heart, the four-box business model is a framework for generating the right questions and assumptions, for organizing and categorizing them in a constructive way, and for implementing, testing, and learning about them in the right order. As we walk through jobs, customer value propositions, profit formulas, and key resources and processes in detail in this chapter and the next, keep in mind that business model innovation is an iterative journey. You may need to move back and forth between the boxes before you come up with the right design that makes all four components work together correctly.

It bears repeating that my point here is about *new* business model creation, not extensions of your current model, or a competitor's, or what everybody else in the industry is doing, as comforting as those approaches always are. This is about the pursuit of game-changing, transformative new growth opportunities, and that pursuit starts with finding important, *unfulfilled* jobs, the first challenge in seizing your white space with business model innovation. This is hard because it often requires looking at your market in a new way.

Nothing is more natural, or more difficult to stop doing, than thinking about the market from the inside out—that is, from the perspective of your own company and your existing products and services. But abandoning the inside-out viewpoint is exactly what you need to do. Remember, we're talking about unmet jobs, which by definition are those your company is *not* filling, perhaps to customers it's not serving. You must give up any conviction you may hold that after successfully delivering your products or services to your existing customers for so long a time you necessarily know all their unmet jobs. Essentially, you should be thinking not like a corporate executive but like an entrepreneur, as if you had not yet sold anything to anyone.

So let's start at the beginning, with the search for an important job a real customer needs to do. I'm sure lots of people have already admonished you to be customer-centric. But what does that really mean?

DISCOVERING THE CUSTOMER'S JOBS

To explain, let's consider a case study.[1] A dental device company I'll call DentCo had carved out a profitable niche with a disruptive technology that broke the skills barrier to consumption. The product allowed general-practice dentists to perform a tooth-straightening procedure that once only orthodontic specialists could do. When competitors started offering similar products at much lower prices, DentCo faced a choice: It could engage in a price war that would devalue the entire market, or it could find another way to counter the opposition. DentCo turned to its customers to figure out its next step.

Most companies in DentCo's situation would begin their market analysis by asking the dental practitioner (either directly or through a market study): "What attributes do you seek in a dental product?" This is called the *needs-based* or *voice-of-the-customer* approach. This seems like a sensible way to be customer-centric but it's really not, for two reasons. First, asking customers what they need from your products tends to elicit predictable answers that relate to your products, such as "less expensive," "less invasive," "easier to use," or "more features." Second, a needs-based approach typically segments the target market according to attributes like product features or demographics that don't necessarily align with jobs customers might need to do. That approach either lumps together individuals who want different jobs to be done or, more rarely, separates groups that actually need the same job done. When DentCo originally defined its market segments demographically as general practitioners and orthodontists, it created such "phantom market segments."

Not surprisingly, companies like this approach. It's relatively easy to collect data on products and demographic segments, and needs-based questions reinforce what incumbents do best—create sustaining product innovations (like dental products with more bells and whistles, in DentCo's case). If DentCo sets out to meet the "needs" of these phantom segments, it will continue to push its current products and start a price-and-features war with its competitors.

I believe needs-based analysis is the wrong approach to conceiving of transformative, growth-generating customer value propositions. To become truly customer-centric, you must stop asking your customers "What do you need?" and start asking them "What are you trying to get done?"[2] This is the question that will set you down the road to a jobs-based approach.

When DentCo asks dentists and orthodontists what they are trying to get done during the course of their workday, that question yields a very different set of market segments and some real answers. To start, DentCo realizes that *all* of its customers want to build a successful practice. That may sound obvious, but it upends phantom segment thinking. It's an important indication that instead of being rigidly separated by specialty all dental practitioners have much in common. As DentCo digs deeper in asking jobs-based questions, it learns what building a successful practice truly means: offering patients the most current care, managing a successful business, and establishing a reputation. Through the course of asking what gets in the way of accomplishing these jobs, DentCo identifies the major barrier to consumption of existing solutions for these jobs: time. New products and procedures that would fulfill the job of building a successful practice require new skills and time to train staff members. And to dentists and orthodontists, time is money, since they are typically paid by procedure, no matter how long it takes.

Now DentCo possesses a truly constructive understanding of its market: What it needs is a value proposition that centers on convenience, one that can help dentists and orthodontists deliver the most current level of care to their patients while minimizing the time required to adopt new technologies. Armed with this customer insight, DentCo can avoid a ruinous price war with competitors. Instead of adding more features and functions to its products, DentCo can develop a suite of value-added offerings that satisfies the true job-to-be-done for the large general market of all dental practitioners. That could include a time-saving expert clinical support hotline, an online forum for sharing best practices, and a staff-training program, all in customizable product bundles. Employing the four-box framework, DentCo can now begin to determine whether it can deliver these new services and capabilities with its current business model or if it needs to create a new one to capture this opportunity.

Focusing on the job-to-be-done gets at the real root of consumer decision making. In his book *The Innovator's Solution*, Clayton Christensen aptly illustrates the concept with the example of a fast-food company trying to improve sales of its milkshakes.[3] Initially, its marketers did exactly what they shouldn't have done—defined the market in terms of its product (milkshakes) and then segmented it further by profiling the demographic characteristics and personalities of the customers who frequently bought them. The marketers then invited representatives from these phantom segments in for a focus group, further intensifying their inside-out orientation by asking the group to evaluate the existing product and—even worse—supplying categories of answers by inquiring whether it should be thicker or more chocolatey or cheaper or chunkier. Participants gave clear answers, and the company made changes accordingly.

After the corresponding improvements failed to increase sales, though, the company brought in a new researcher. He made no assumptions about customer segments and didn't ask anyone for suggestions about improving the current product. Instead, he spent a long day watching people in one of the restaurants to see what they were trying to get done when they "hired" a milkshake. He noted what time it was when each milkshake was bought, which other products were bought with it, who was with the customers when they made their purchases, and whether people drank the shakes on the premises or sped off in their cars before downing them.

Seen from the job-to-be-done perspective, it turned out purchasers hire milkshakes to fulfill two distinct jobs, and the primary user in both cases is the same person—a working father. In the morning, Dad is rushing to get to work and doesn't have time to eat breakfast before he hits the road for his long daily commute. But in the afternoon or the evening, Dad takes the kids out for a fast-food dinner and wants to reward them for good behavior with a milkshake after their meal (as we all know, the official *Rule Book of Kids* says that the most important thing in the world is a treat at the end of the day).

These two distinct jobs dictate two different solutions. In the morning, Dad is using the milkshake to overcome his hunger and, as an experience, to alleviate some of the boredom of his tedious commute. He wants the shake to fill time as well as his belly, so he prefers it to be highly viscous, and perhaps have chunks of fruit to make it and the drive more interesting. In the evening, Dad wants the kids to hurry up, so he prefers a less viscous and fruit-free product that they can slurp up pretty quickly. None of that information could ever be obtained by asking people how they liked the milkshake, no matter how marketers sliced and diced the segments, since the same person needed two different jobs done.

Ideally, maintaining a focus on the jobs customers need done is not something you hire a marketer to do when your sales start flagging. That knowledge should spring from paying close attention in a more ongoing and systematic way to the jobs your customers are having trouble fulfilling. Hilti, for example, would never have spotted its opportunity to escape commoditization in the tool market if it had not already been in constant touch with customers through regular surveys, both formal and informal, that asked not only about product performance but also about worksite needs and desires. Hilti also sends videographers and observers to worksites to watch how its customers use its products and conduct their daily tasks. Had the company simply asked customers what they wanted or needed from its tools, it would probably have gotten various replies like "more reliable tools" or "cheaper tools."

A jobs-based approach applies as much to business-to-business companies and to multistakeholder situations as it does to direct consumers. DentCo could, for instance, build an even stronger offering, and eventually a more robust business model, by deeply considering the jobs of the patient, third-party payers, and regulators—all of whom share a common interest in the jobs-to-be-done of the practitioner—and then building an offering that accounts for various jobs.

SATISFYING EMOTIONAL AND SOCIAL JOBS

It's critical when searching for unfilled jobs-to-be-done to realize that you must think not only about the *functional* aspects of a job but also about its *social* and *emotional* aspects—which together make up the experience that customers desire in accomplishing the job.[4] Hindustan Unilever, for instance, realized that the Shakti Ammas would be more successful if they were able to deliver something more valuable to village life than branded products. So as the initiative went forward, the company found it could help boost their social standing by reinforcing the illness-prevention aspects of personal hygiene. This made the women more than salespeople; they became purveyors of important social benefits.

Shai Agassi realized early on in the development of the value proposition for Better Place that no matter how much people wanted to be environmentally conscious, they were not willing to give up their emotional relationship with their cars to do so. You couldn't, say, ask them to drive a three-wheeled plastic electro-cycle just to save gas; they wouldn't buy something they didn't feel was socially acceptable. They were also range-anxious, meaning that although most people drove less than twenty miles a day, they were generally uncomfortable buying a car that clocks fewer than three hundred miles before needing to be refueled.[5] Better Place developed its business model to explicitly address these respective social and emotional aspects of the job-to-be-done.

These jobs are less tangible and thus harder to pin down, yet they remain important, and sometimes critical, considerations in the development of a new business model. In fashion, for example, social and emotional jobs dominate customer-purchasing decisions. The job of fashion is to "Help me feel good about the way I look." It has functional aspects—"Provide something appropriate to my body type, in colors that match my complexion"—but far more significant social and emotional ones— "Help me fit in, look current, attract a mate, feel confident and sexy, and impress others." By focusing on these aspects of his customers' job-to-be-done, Spaniard Amancio Ortega transformed the business model of his retail chain, Zara, and created what Louis Vuitton fashion director Daniel Piette called "possibly the most innovative and devastating retailer in the world."[6]

In the 1980s, mass media exposed consumers around the world to diverse ways of dressing, and tastes changed rapidly. A new video from a trendsetter like pop star Madonna or rock band Duran Duran, for instance, could be seen everywhere in days, igniting a fashion craze that might last a summer or a year—no one could predict. At the same time, however, the fashion industry itself was slowing down. Globalization began to open access to new markets of cheap labor. To be more profitable, most fashion houses disaggregated internal functions like design and marketing from fabric sourcing, manufacturing, and finishing. Since each step in the value chain required additional time to coordinate, designers found themselves having to finalize looks up to a year in advance of the selling season. So while customers were demanding faster and fresher fashions, designers were pushing last year's looks.

Recognizing this dynamic, Ortega envisioned a new type of company, one that addressed the important social jobs by creating "instant fashions": clothes that could be designed and brought to market as fast as demand arose.[7]

Zara needed to fundamentally redesign its key resources and processes—and integrate them in an entirely different way—to deliver its new customer value proposition. It employed advanced automated systems to tightly integrate its retail, inventory, and design processes. It built a state-of-the-art communications system that turned store managers into trend spotters and linked them to in-house designers. It assembled most of its clothes locally and built a just-in-time shipping system capable of delivering goods to every store twice a week. Zara used the best technology of the day to build an integrated supply chain that could produce garments virtually on demand and ship only the number of items required. With this efficient and responsive operation, Zara could deliver new fashions to market not fifteen months after they were designed, or even fifteen weeks, but in as little as fifteen days.[8]

Guided by the social and emotional aspects of its customers' job-to-be-done, Zara reshaped virtually every part of its business model and became a leading global fashion business. It grew spectacularly by adopting an outside-in approach that better served its market, delivering a level of customization and freshness never before seen in the industry. And it did so largely before the information revolution and the Internet made customer-centricity a much easier approach.

THE INTERNET AND CUSTOMER CENTRICITY

The Internet—and Web 2.0 tools in particular—now give businesses an unprecedented ability to deeply understand their customers. Companies can now connect directly with customers and potential markets to learn highly specific information about them, abrogating the need to rely on phantom segments, trend spotters, or needs-based analysis. More important, customers can connect with companies to demand what they want.

Rising apparel maker Threadless built a unique business model to exploit this new reality using social networking technology to sell T-shirts entirely designed by its customers. Threadless accepts design submissions on its Web site from its rapidly growing community of amateur designers and young trendsetters and lets them vote on the products they want to buy. It can then manufacture popular designs within hours using mass-customization technology, fulfilling the job of keeping its customers' fashions up to the minute through the efficiency of a just-in-time supply chain.[9]

By giving the customer direct control of the company's product design, Threadless has built a thriving community of consumers who feel an ownership stake in its brand. Producing a predetermined demand keeps costs low and margins above 30 percent. And because community members tell it precisely which shirts to make, Threadless never has a flop; every product eventually sells out. "Threadless completely blurs that line of who is a

producer and who is a consumer," Harvard Business School professor Karim Lakhani told *Inc.* magazine. "The customers end up
playing a critical role across all its operations: idea generation,
marketing, sales forecasting. All that has been distributed."[10]

The Threadless model illustrates the power of the customer in
a networked world. Success now more than ever flows from the
outside in, from the market to the company. Incumbents therefore need to think creatively about how they can cultivate discern-
ing insights into the full range of functional, social, and emotional
customer jobs-to-be-done.

DESIGNING THE NEW CVP

Having identified an important job-to-be-done for a customer,
you need to create a blueprint of the business model that will satisfy it. Designing a new model begins, of course, with the customer value proposition—the offering that addresses the job at a
prescribed price. As you may recall from chapter 2, a comprehensive customer value proposition combines in an offering not only
what is sold (product and/or service) but *how* it is sold. That
includes the ways in which a product or service is made available
(access) and the ways the customer can pay for it (the payment
scheme). And also remember, the more important the job, the
better the match between the offering and this job, and (usually)
the lower the price of the offering, the greater the overall value
generated for the customer.

I recommend you begin by thinking in the most basic of
terms. With the job-to-be-done firmly in mind, ask yourself: Can
I fulfill it with a product? A service? A combination of the two? In
considering the offering as a product, continue to ask questions
like: Will it be a durable or a consumable? Will its feature set
be limited or extensive? Will it require light or heavy customer
support? Will we supply it directly or through suppliers? Will

customers need to access it frequently or infrequently?[11] Questions about the nature of pricing and payments are similarly basic: Will customers pay in cash or by financing? Will the price be fixed or variable? Will they pay once or in installments? To visualize these choices, I like to think of each as a lever that you can push up toward one choice or down toward the other. A final offering can, of course, fall somewhere between the two extremes, but I find this exercise to be a helpful starting place for thinking broadly about possibilities. The following figures illustrate a

FIGURE 25

The customer value proposition formula

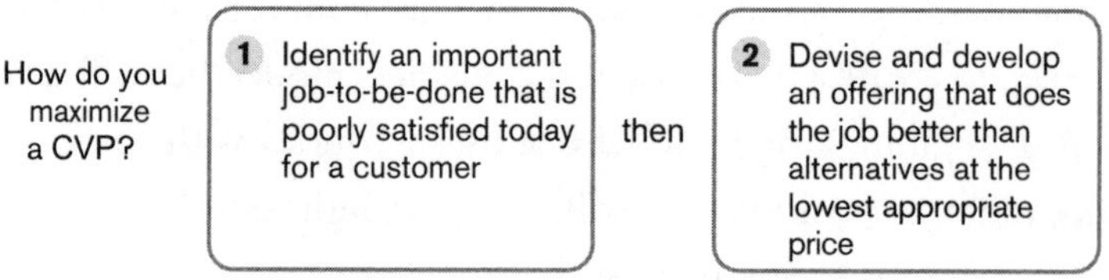

How do you maximize a CVP?

1 Identify an important job-to-be-done that is poorly satisfied today for a customer

then

2 Devise and develop an offering that does the job better than alternatives at the lowest appropriate price

FIGURE 26

Thinking expansively about different CVP components

CVP component	Key questions from the customer's perspective
Offering	• Does the offering satisfy my job-to-be-done? • Does it offer the right trade-offs? • Are the elements that matter most good enough for what I need?
Access	• How do I get the offering? • From whom do I get the offering? • How often will I need to purchase the offering?
Payment scheme	• What am I paying for? (pay per unit, pay per use, pay when value is added) • When do I pay? (pay up front, subscription, etc.) • What is the form of payment? (cash, credit, finance, exchange)

range of top-level characteristics that define the basic structure of most CVPs.

As an illustration, consider Dow Corning's model once again. Before it developed the Xiameter low-cost business model, the company's customers bought a combination of silicone products and technical service directly through a highly trained, specialized sales force. They chose from a wide array of silicone product offerings and had an almost unlimited choice of volume options. Ultimately, they purchased a customized offering to suit their unique needs and negotiated individual price and financing contracts. Xiameter sought to serve a new price-driven customer job with a CVP that flipped the levers to the other side. It limited order sizes and the number of product offerings, all of which were

FIGURE 27

A sampling of product/service levers

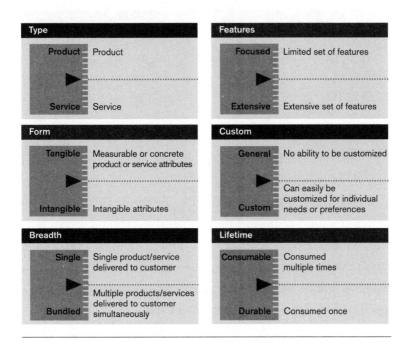

FIGURE 28

Sample access levers

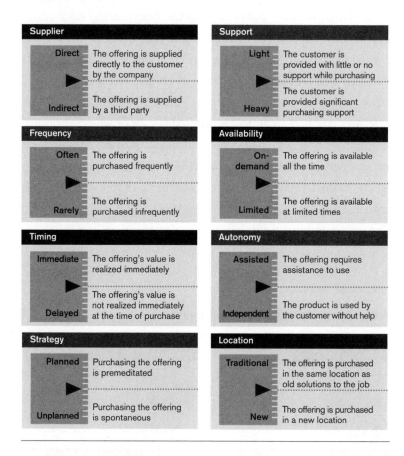

accessible only online. Lead times, pricing, and payment terms all were fixed as well.

In the case of Hilti, the levers flipped the other way, moving from a commodity product to a high-end service and from a generalized product to a highly customized one tailored to the requirements of the individual construction-site customer. Access switched from light support to heavy service and support available practically anytime. The payment system moved from pay-for-product to pay-for-service, with payment now being made in monthly installments.

FIGURE 29

Sample payment levers

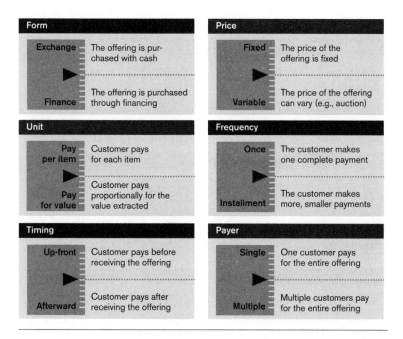

Dozens of levers could be considered when designing your CVP, depending on your particular context, but to begin focus on those you deem most crucial to the offering. Hindustan Unilever, for instance, zeroed in on the need for a lot of customer support right from the start in the form of training and education of the Shakti Ammas.

DEVISING THE PROFIT FORMULA

Once you have an idea of your CVP, it's time to devise possible ways your company can make money delivering it. In this regard, I advocate for a very different approach than the one most companies use when contemplating new business development.

In a customary business development process, executives work in a deliberate, somewhat mechanistic way. They assess the facts

FIGURE 30

Contrasting offerings

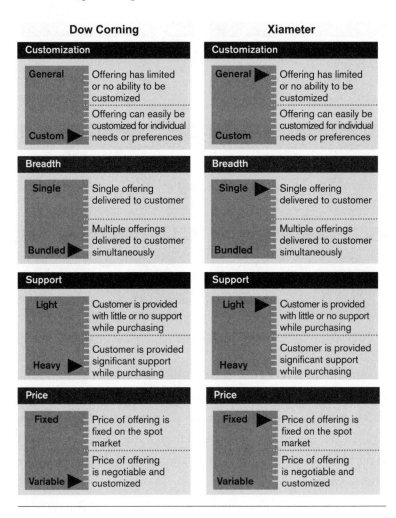

and assumptions about the future business environment and then project a growth plan that falls within the core enterprise's usual way of making money. When a new business idea emerges that seems to support this plan and conform to the existing financial model, it gets serious consideration and perhaps a green light. But if the idea calls for a different way of making money, the finance people tend to put on their green visors, sharpen their pencils, and try to graft the established profit formula onto the developing new venture. If the new CVP can't conform to the established overhead structure, margins, rate of return, and so on it often gets killed, a phenomenon I'll revisit in greater detail in chapter 8.

It is far better to take a flexible approach to business model design that keeps the focus squarely on the job and on value creation for the customer, not on the profit formula. To that aim, I suggest working up a range of financial projections appropriate to the new CVP that represent various ways value could be delivered to the company. The goal is to establish a set of reasonable assumptions that can be tested and modified during implementation in an iterative fashion.

The best you can do at this stage is to develop reasonable assumptions about possible combinations of resources (people, technology, facilities, and so on) to deploy that imply different unit margin assumptions in support of the value proposition. Different volume or quantity assumptions can be developed but cannot be absolutely confirmed in a market that doesn't yet exist. So the right financial approach hinges on assumptions that can only be tested during implementation. In other words, at this point, you should be taking a much looser approach to making money.

"A loose approach to making money?" you might be thinking. "You must be crazy."

But take a moment to consider it. First, it's a given that the blueprints you design at this stage are likely to be wrong, or more precisely, they'll probably evolve substantially before you get the formula right. But business, being business, tends to be numbers-driven. So when executives see numbers that look good, they want to lock them in and then do whatever it takes to achieve them. This approach can lead to all sorts of deviations from the goal of fulfilling customer jobs: Offerings will be redesigned, superfluous features added, and essential ones eliminated; resources will be allocated according to short-term financial objectives rather than according to how they serve the CVP. If you finalize a profit formula too early or, worse, are compelled to conform financials to the core business's profit formula, then when things change—as they inevitably will—you'll end up making wrongheaded compromises.

Moreover, although it's necessary to arrive at a focused CVP during the blueprinting process, the financials to support it— How much will it cost to make? What is our unit margin or the volume we need to cover our overhead costs? What kind of profit do we need to commit to it?—typically involve a great many assumptions. As understanding of the new business develops, the choices contingent on the greatest number of assumptions will tend to change the most. Executives who don't understand this are often too quick to kill new initiatives that don't hit their projected numbers right away.

The fact is, implementing a new business model is mostly about managing assumptions. To manage assumptions, you must define them clearly, then test them during the implementation process. That will give you the evidence you need to confirm those assumptions or find out that they are unfounded in some way and adjust accordingly. If in the course of considering profit formulas you develop several potential avenues of profitability, you will be better able to adapt to the needs of the CVP without derailing or compromising the offering. This is what I mean when I advocate for a loose approach to making money. Having a range of choices that you can pursue intelligently as the new model evolves will help you converge on the ultimate profit formula and resist falling back into old habits.

To work up that range of choices, begin by brainstorming as many financial scenarios as possible. One way to help jump-start your creative juices is to think by analogy—to consider how the model for an existing business in another industry might be applied to your context. Better Place, for instance, is applying a cell phone service model to electric cars. Apple's iPod/iTunes model and Amazon's Kindle e-book apply the reverse of King Gillette's blades-and-razor model to digital media. Not every new game-changing business model must be cut from whole cloth; sometimes it's enough to employ a familiar one in a new way.

FIGURE 31

Business model analogies

Type	Example	Description
Affinity club	MBNA	Partner with membership associations and other affinity groups to offer a product exclusively to its members, exchanging royalties for access to a larger customer base.
Brokerage	Century 21, Orbitz	Bring together and facilitate transactions between buyers and sellers, charging a fee for each successful transaction.
Bundling	Fast-food value meals, iPod/iTunes	Make purchasing simple and more complete by packaging related products together.
Cell phone	Sprint, Better Place	Sell a service through multiple plans featuring a range of prices depending on varying levels of usage.
Crowdsourcing	Wikipedia, YouTube	Outsource tasks to a broad group who contribute content for free in exchange for access to other users' content.
Disintermediation	Dell, WebMD	Deliver directly to the customer a product or service that has traditionally gone through an intermediary.
Fractionalization	Time-sharing condos, NetJets	Allow users to own part of a product but enjoy many of the benefits of full ownership for a fraction of the price.
Freemium	Skype, LinkedIn, Pandora	Offer basic services for free but charge for upgraded or premium services.
Leasing	Xerox, luxury cars, MachineryLink	Make high-margin, high-cost products affordable by having the customer rent rather than buy them.
Low-touch	Southwest, Wal-mart, Xiameter	Offer low-price, low-service version of a traditionally high-end offering.
Negative operating cycle	Amazon	Generate high profits by maintaining low inventory and having the customer pay up front for a product or service to be delivered in the future.
Pay-as-you-go	PG&E, metered ISPs	Charge the customer for metered services based on actual usage rates.
Razors/blades	Gillette, personal printers	Offer the higher-margin "razors" for low or no cost to make profits by selling high-volume, low-margin "blades."
Reverse auction	Elance.com, OnForce.com	Set a ceiling price for a product or service and have participants bid the price down.
Reverse razors/blades	iPod/iTunes, Amazon Kindle	Offer the low-margin "blades" at no or low cost to encourage sales of the higher-margin "razors."
Product-to-service	IBM, Hilti, Zipcar	Rather than sell products outright, sell the service the product performs.
Standardization	MinuteClinic	Provide lower cost standardized solutions to problems that once could only be addressed through high-cost customized products or services.
Subscription club	Magazines, Costco, Netflix	Charge the customer a subscription fee to gain access to a product or service.
User communities	Angie's List	Grant members access to a network, generating revenue through membership fees and advertisements.

To fully develop a viable profit formula, you naturally must build an actual profit and loss statement. One very useful tool for working up the projections for a business with a new profit formula is a *reverse income statement*.[12] Rather than start with revenue, as you would with a traditional income statement, arriving at profits by figuring costs and then margins, you create a reverse income statement by starting with a profit goal that answers the question, "How big does the aggregate profit need to be in three to five years for this opportunity to be worthwhile?" Then you work backward toward defining a viable revenue model, cost structure, and unit margin, using the elements of the profit formula described in chapter 2:

- Revenue model (price × quantity)

- Cost structure (direct costs and overhead)

- Target unit margin

- Resource velocity (inventory turns, staff utilization in professional services firms, etc.)

Revenues are figured by estimating the total quantity of the offering that will be sold and then multiplying that by the price required by the CVP. With that estimate of total quantity sold, combined with the cost of the direct materials and labor required per unit, you can determine the associated allocated overhead cost and then confirm the unit margin needed to reach your profit targets. The $2,000 price point of Tata's Nano, for example, required dramatically reducing not only the direct costs of the car but also the nonrecurring costs of design, administration, and other overhead to make the car profitable.

The resulting profit and loss statement represents a set of assumptions about margins, cost structure (including cost of goods sold and marketing and advertising budgets), resource velocity, and the like. In this way, the profit and loss sheet becomes a planning document that helps you build a set of testable assumptions.

Ultimately, with a newly formed customer value proposition and basic profit formula, you are trying to answer two simple questions: Can you tell a story that explains how delivering the new CVP will create strong growth? If so, can you articulate a range of financial scenarios about how you might achieve that success? Each of these scenarios needs to be what musicians call "pure tones." In other words, the options you develop need to be clearly differentiated from each other so that you can clearly analyze the pros and cons of each one.

IDENTIFYING THE KEY RESOURCES AND KEY PROCESSES

In the process of working out a reverse income statement and profit formula, you will naturally begin to identify the key resources and processes needed to deliver the CVP, and you will also begin to make assumptions about their cost, availability, and feasibility. Zara knew that to deliver its clothing to widely dispersed retail locations twice every week and still remain competitive, it would have to cut costs elsewhere in the business model. So it understood that a key process would be its centralized manufacturing-to-shipping value chain.[13] Dow Corning quickly realized that IT infrastructure would be a critical resource for Xiameter and so put its development at the top of the new venture effort. And for Hilti, backroom contract management processes were essential.

But while you will be able to identify some key resources and processes during this early design phase, they will become more important in the implementation phase that follows. That's when you will test them to see if you have selected correctly, if you can tightly integrate them with the other elements of the business model, and if your processes will really work.

Before moving on to the implementation phase of a new business initiative, it's wise to stop and compare its blueprint to the business model of your core enterprise. Identifying points of compatibility and differentiation will help guide the next stage in two critical ways. First, you will see which of the key resources can be taken from (or must be shared with) the core so you can develop a strategy that will allow you to pull them in when you need them. And second, you will be able to identify early on those potential points of conflict where the expectations and habits of the core could interfere with the new effort's success, understanding just how much business model change will be required.

7

Implementing the Model

The characteristic of scientific progress is our
knowing that we did not know.

—Gaston Bachelard

A great business model blueprint is a powerful first step in seizing your white space. But making the leap from the theoretical blueprint to the working business doesn't happen all at once. It's is a process of controlled experimentation that proceeds in small steps. Hypotheses are put forward and tested, and the lessons learned are used to make the necessary adjustments as you go forward. In this way, long before much is risked, you will discover if the new model won't work in practice or how it needs to change so that it will.

This is how I use the term *implementation*: an effort largely focused on testing and validating assumptions while integrating the key resources and processes required to deliver on the customer value proposition and the profit formula. Implementation should be pursued in three stages: incubation, acceleration, and

FIGURE 32

Stages of business model implementation

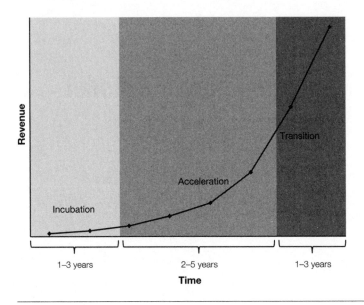

transition.[1] Incubation should be focused on establishing profitability, but it's critical not to put pressure on the project to reap
revenues at any great pace until the acceleration stages and in
many cases real, large-scale revenues won't accrue until the transition stage.

INCUBATION

Incubation is the process of identifying the assumptions most
critical to the success of the business proposition and then testing
them in a targeted and orderly manner to quickly prove or dis-
prove their viability and by extension the viability of the new initiative itself. At this stage, creative problem solving and a
discovery-driven approach to project planning are critical skills.[2]
The immediate goal here isn't necessarily business success; it

is *new learning*. Testing that delivers clear answers should be encouraged, even if they come from failures.

"For every one of our failures, we had spreadsheets that looked awesome," jokes Scott Cook, founder of accounting software pioneer Intuit.[3] As the leader of a highly innovative company, Cook learned through experience the value of focused testing. A team once brought Cook a proposal to create a business that paired accountants who had available time on their hands with those who had more work than they could handle, essentially transforming a local service market into an internationally networked one. Accountants, the team assumed, were very good at counting but not as skilled at marketing or acquiring new clients. The team had gone quite deep in its analysis, producing detailed spreadsheets—based on all sorts of noncritical assumptions—about the idea's potential profitability. It seemed to be a brilliant idea, but the team had no hard data.

"Instead of working nine months to build the whole service," Cook says, "I asked, 'Can you find a way to test quickly the supply hypothesis?' So the team hacked together something in three weeks—had humans doing stuff behind the scenes instead of the computer—and sent a little test mailing to fifty thousand accountants. By the fifth week they had proved—at virtually no cost—that there were good accountants sitting unused."[4] And they kept learning. The team continued to develop the project, launching one piece every few weeks, following this test-and-learn approach.

Typically, new business initiatives fail because the people responsible for them take assumptions to be fact. They don't work hard enough or systematically enough to identify and validate critical assumptions before either committing large resources to the business proposition or walking away. Managers need to *test early, test cheaply, and test often*. Investing a little to learn a lot helps overcome the uncertainty of new business development by enabling managers to modify plans in response to new knowledge.

"Fast testing is risk reducing," concludes Cook, "and most people are happy pursuing risk-reducing behavior. Once the value of this approach becomes apparent to all, it becomes part of your innovation culture. New teams, rather than commit large resources to vague planning, begin to ask early on how they can test their key hypotheses."[5]

To successfully incubate a new business you must identify a *foothold market*, a small geographic region or customer group that will serve as the low-cost laboratory. Preferably familiar or otherwise friendly, the market nevertheless needs to be representative of the larger target market you intend ultimately to pursue.[6] Hindustan Unilever tested the Shakti Initiative in Andhra Pradesh, a state in southern India, starting with just seventeen women, slowly expanding the number as the company learned what it needed to succeed. Better Place identified a favorable foothold market in Israel, a relatively small transportation island with a vested interest in the project's success. Hilti worked out the resources and processes of its white-space play with a few large clients in its base market of Switzerland before slowly rolling its model out worldwide. Incubating a new business in your white space is filled with uncertainty, but it needn't be filled with risk. Foothold markets allow for safe, low-cost, structured testing that yields demonstrable results.

Most critically—and I cannot stress this enough—you must keep the incubation effort free of interference from the core and the way it operates. "Part of the creative challenge is not having too many controls," says Netflix founder and CEO Reed Hastings. "We manage new innovation through context, through values and influence, rather than control. We talk about *supporting* innovation, rather than *managing, controlling,* or *proceduralizing* it, because it's so creative."[7] This is another way of saying that incubation should be oriented toward deploying key resources rather than refining processes.

A Tale of Two Low-Cost Carriers

While incubating a new business model, constant attention must be paid to the interrelationship of all its key elements and their ability to integrate harmoniously in support of the customer value proposition. Models whose elements don't mesh well almost inevitably fail.

Consider, for instance, the examples of Southwest Airlines and Delta's Song Airlines, two low-cost airline players that met with vastly different results. Southwest Airlines is generally credited with starting the low-cost airline revolution. Its story has been told many times. But viewing it through the lens of the four-box business model framework shows how important internal consistency is to Southwest's success.

At its inception, Southwest targeted regional commuter customers whose needs were being ignored by the big carriers. These were mainly Texas residents who were taking the bus between cities like Austin and Dallas and couldn't afford air travel. They were nonconsumers, and Southwest astutely realized it was competing not against other airlines but against bus travel. It set out to satisfy commuters' job-to-be-done by providing faster transportation at a nearly comparable price. This CVP put necessary constraints on Southwest's profit formula. To deliver revolutionary low prices, it would have to keep margins low. To make money at these margins, it would need to keep direct costs and overhead low and resource velocity high. It would have to find ways to get more turns from its capital equipment.

As the company began to develop the key elements of its model, it made choices to support these requirements. For instance, Southwest adopted a direct sales model for tickets, eliminating travel agent fees, which also put payments in the company's hands more quickly. Customer service could be high-touch (friendly behavior is cheap), but expensive extras like food and entertainment were trimmed or eliminated. On the resource front, the airline chose to use a single type of plane to streamline repair and main-tenance costs and relied heavily on electronic systems to run sales channels. Externally, Southwest chose to fly into secondary air-ports, whose lower gate fees reduced operating costs. It also nego-tiated industry-rule-breaking profit-sharing contracts with its pilots' union, thus trimming another traditional source of high costs.[8] Finally, it entered into long-term contracts for fuel.

These key resources all supported both the CVP and the profit formula. Secondary airports and standardized maintenance procedures—aided by a point-to-point routing system that decreased the waiting times associated with industry dominant hub-and-spoke routing—produced industry-leading turnaround times, maximizing asset velocity by keeping planes flying a greater per-centage of the time.[9] And Southwest's decision to do away with reserved seating and institute a first-come, first-served approach got passengers on and off planes more quickly. Taken together, these choices formed a cohesive model that reinforced South-west's CVP and led to great success.

Years later, legacy carrier Delta attempted to enter the low-cost travel business. It launched Song, aimed at "discount divas," female leisure flyers who wanted the convenience and affordabil-ity of a low-cost carrier coupled with a sense of style. In addition to serving a slightly refined customer segment, Song's CVP differ-entiator was a "hip" approach to travel. It was a white-space-within play for Delta, but the company failed to recognize it as such. Like Southwest, Song's profit formula relied on low mar-gins, low cost drivers, and high resource velocity, a strategy that might have worked but for the incongruity of the other elements in its model.

Emulating Southwest, Delta chose a single type of aircraft fly-ing point-to-point routes, which it hoped would result in faster turnaround times and higher resource velocity. But to serve its divas, it retained reserved boarding and lots of frills like organic food, custom cocktails, personal entertainment systems, designer attendant uniforms, and an in-flight exercise program, all of which either added costs or slowed turnaround by increasing restocking and cleaning time. Fun, fashionable service is not fast, efficient service. These tensions in the model were difficult to reconcile. Flying to primary airports further increased costs and impeded resource velocity, as Song jets struggled to move quickly on crowded runways amid busy infrastructures.

The factor that was perhaps most destructive to the success of the model, however, was that Delta, in an effort to avoid alienating its unions, saddled Song with its existing pilots, crews, and machinists. All were protected by high-cost union contracts, and they were unaccustomed to the resource velocity required to make the Song model work. The core culture was hard to change and caused further tensions in the system. These inherent conflicts ultimately proved fatal.

Southwest's and Song's business models both had strong customer value propositions serving specific jobs-to-be-done, and both featured differentiators designed to serve those jobs (you might question the discount-divas concept, but at least it was clearly defined in Delta executives' minds). But Southwest perfected its model in small foothold markets before gradually expanding to national service, whereas Delta bet the bank on a business model whose elements, it turned out, weren't well integrated and therefore did not support Song's CVP—and its initiative failed.

Profit Before Revenue Growth

Early in the incubation process, the business model framework helps to identify the new value propositions that have the greatest chance of success and weed out those that contain fatal flaws or inconsistencies. Just as important as testing assumptions is correctly defining what will constitute success and how you will

FIGURE 33

Success of Southwest Airlines

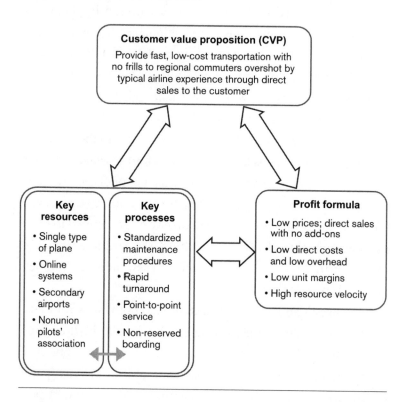

measure it. Some of the best-conceived initiatives have gone down in flames from such common errors as an overeager push for scale, overinvestment in imperfect suppositions, and a lack of patience with a process that needs time as its friend.

Transformational business models should demonstrate the success of their fundamentals fairly quickly by delivering value to the customer and profits to the company early on. Hindustan Unilever was able to predict the eventual success of the Shakti Initiative on the basis of early profit accrued from just a few dozen women. Xiameter started filling the production pipeline and clearing profit almost immediately after it refined the stringent

FIGURE 34

Failure of Song Airlines

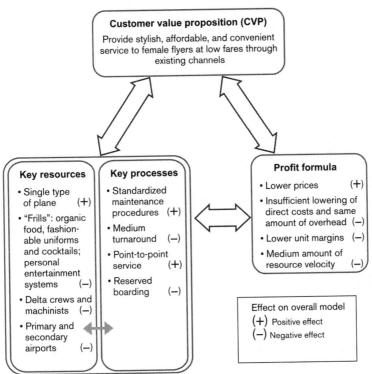

business rules needed to serve its commodity market. The evidence of profitability demonstrated early on by Hilti's initial eight customers gave Marco Meyrat and the other company executives confidence in the tool-leasing service. That granted them the patience to scale up in a measured way in their initial foothold market of Switzerland and beyond.

This is one of the great benefits of applying the business model framework to new business development. By articulating the basic framework and focusing early and explicitly on the initial key assumptions that define that framework, it becomes relatively straightforward to identify and evaluate proper metrics for success. A clear definition, combined with the right approach to business model blueprinting and implementation, provides the structure you need to significantly reduce the investment and execution risk of ventures in your white space. Reduced risk means reduced fear, and as the fear of the unknown subsides, your white space becomes a more reasonable place to explore.

Successful incumbents may initially dislike revisiting the uncertainty they have worked so hard to banish. But you must learn to manage the paradox of embracing uncertainty while methodically working to stamp it out. You need to build tolerance for initial failure. In 1999, for example, Amazon wanted to expand the resources it offered customers. Seeing eBay's popularity, it introduced an auction model to engage third-party sellers in the Amazon experience. The experiment was widely viewed as an abject failure at the time, but in fact, it was an important step in an emergent strategy that Amazon pursued to great eventual success. "The basic thought was: 'Look, we have this Web site where we sell things, and we want to have vast selection,'" says CEO Jeff Bezos, relating a story he often shares at company events:

> One of the ways to get vast selection is to invite other sellers—third parties—onto our Web site to participate alongside us and make it into a win-win situation. So we did auctions, but we didn't like the results. . . . Next we created zShops, which was fixed-price selling, but still parked those third parties in separate parts of the store. If a third-party seller had a used copy of *Harry Potter* to sell, it would have its own detail page, rather than having its availability listed right next to the new copy. We still didn't like the results we got. It was when we went to the single-detail-page model that our third-party business really took off. Now, if we're offering a certain digital camera and you're a seller with the same camera to sell, you can go

right on our own detail page, right next to our product, and underbid us. And if you do, we will put you in the "buy" box, which is on that page.[10]

As assumptions are tested, success or failure increases the knowledge in the system. As the enterprise gains traction and turns the corner toward viability, demonstrable knowledge takes over. At that point, clearly defining the metrics of success gives you a clear path toward achieving it, better enabling the nascent initiative to absorb the inevitable early failures along the way.

ACCELERATION

Once you've proven that a new model is viable through a well-staged incubation effort, it's time to step on the accelerator. The knowledge side of the equation is substantially higher now, so here you focus less on experimentation and more on setting up repeatable processes to make your business profitable. Acceleration begins by refining and standardizing processes, establishing the business rules that govern them, and defining metrics that chart continuing success. Over time, these rules and metrics get internalized as norms; people think of them as "the way things get done." Imposing such controls maintains quality and customer satisfaction as the business expands. These must be monitored and refined as the new business reaches each stage of growth to make sure the various business activities involved are still in harmony with one another.

Shifting from incubation to acceleration means moving from footholds to broad market adoption. Zara became one of the world's fastest-growing and most successful clothing retailers in part because of the way it patiently accelerated its business model. In the first fifteen years of its life, Zara expanded only in Spain and established strong profitability in this home foothold market.

It did not open its first international store until 1988, and then only in nearby Oporto, Portugal. The following year, it crossed the pond to the United States but found little success there.[11] The company realized that the challenges of internationally scaling up a model based on centralized manufacturing and control required significant adjustments to both its value chain and profit formula. Specifically, it needed to design a highly advanced integrated communications system that would allow its vertically integrated production model to extend successfully to remote locations. But because Zara's investment in this overseas test was minimal, it was able to bring to bear the key resources and evolve the model to develop the needed capability.

In 1990, Zara entered the nearby French market and found greater success. It quickly began adding new stores in major city centers throughout the country.[12] Each market provided further opportunity to experiment and adjust. "Trial and error is a key part of our model," says a company spokesperson.[13]

Zara's patience for growth and willingness to explore different ownership paradigms—company-owned superstores on the Continent, franchises in Russia, partnerships elsewhere—helped it understand what its innovative model was ideally suited to do, and just as important, what it was not. Over time, it streamlined processes and concentrated acceleration efforts where they would be most likely to succeed.

Hindustan Unilever had a similar stop-and-go experience with its Shakti model. It successfully grew the business from twenty-eight hundred to forty-five thousand Shakti Ammas in just a couple of years, but as it contemplated the next stage of growth, it identified key processes that needed refinement if they were to support the much larger scale it envisioned.[14] Hindustan Unilever kept the company at forty-five thousand representatives for some two years while it adjusted the model to correct the logistical challenges of higher volume and create new educational tools suited to a more diverse group. In 2008, it accelerated toward its target of one hundred thousand Shakti Ammas by 2010.[15]

Both companies grew intelligently while controlling risk. Throughout their acceleration processes, they vigilantly monitored how the elements of their models were holding up and working together, and they were able to change their rules and metrics, speed up, or slow down as necessary to protect and perfect the new businesses.

TRANSITION

The final stage of implementation applies only to incumbent enterprises. It addresses the question: Can the new business be reintegrated into the core or must it remain a separate unit in order to thrive?

I believe that the highest likelihood of success accrues to efforts that are kept fully separate from the core from the beginning of the strategy development process until well into the life of the new business. Most companies operate in a culture of advocacy: Units or silos protect their turf and push for what they want and need. Such infighting can crush attempts at business model innovation. "A large segment will always dominate a small one," says Terry Kelly, president and CEO of outdoor apparel and plastics technology company W. L. Gore & Associates. "You must think carefully about dividing and segmenting so that emerging opportunities are not stifled. Leaders must determine how to divide in order to multiply."[16]

Determining the ultimate disposition of a newly developed business model should, of course, be guided by management's judgment about the operating conditions that will give it the greatest chance of long-term success. But all too often a model's unique characteristics are overlooked in a knee-jerk desire to consolidate operations. As a set of general guidelines, a new business model should probably be separated out from an existing business unit when:

- It calls for a significantly different set of business rules and accompanying metrics, which will evolve into significantly different norms

- It requires a distinct brand with a very different promise than a core brand to fulfill its CVP

- It tends to be disruptive to the core business model (that is, it makes money with a much lower margin) and requires a much lower overhead structure and/or a much higher resource velocity

It may be possible to reintegrate a new business into the core if:

- It differentiates itself mainly in its resources and processes, but its profit formula is substantially similar or provides greater unit margins

- It enhances the core brand in some significant fashion

- It can transform and improve the core

As we saw in chapter 3, Xiameter discovered it needed autonomy from Dow Corning's core operations very early in its incubation process when Don Sheets set up his experimental war game to gauge how existing staff and systems would react to the requirements of the new CVP. "The results were not positive," says Sheets, "but it was the best thing that could have happened. If we had gotten caught up renegotiating and attempting to agree on everything with regard to the Xiameter brand, we'd still be waiting to launch it. Many efforts, when they lose a war game like that, are folded or significantly redirected. It just made it clear to me how we needed to be separate."[17]

Hindustan Unilever paved the way for the possible integration of Shakti by accruing all early profits to the core and having Shakti employees work side by side with their HUL colleagues. Even so, the parent company still needed to evaluate how well the initiative would survive in the core. Once Shakti had grown to sufficient scale to prove its worth and not get smothered, Hindustan Unilever considered whether to reintegrate it into its rural distribution unit. Company leaders felt strongly that the Shakti model was the future of rural development for the company, believing the model would spur transformational growth in that market. They determined that to continue to grow the unit would benefit from the added resources of the core. Though there were clashes of organizational culture during the transition, the model has so far been successful because the ground had been well prepared ahead of time and the company culture valued entrepreneurial achievement.

Hilti devoted little serious consideration to whether the new business model could be nurtured and operated successfully within the core or would need to be a separate unit. But since the new model called for higher margins than the old, integration made sense. And it didn't hurt that Hilti had a history of successful transformations: Its adaptable organizational culture was uniquely suited to embracing change.

For the purposes of explicating the business model innovation process, I'm calling transition the last stage, but integration issues must in fact be considered throughout the incubation and acceleration stages. Building a successful new model requires that incumbents constantly test and evaluate it against their existing business model to see what tensions arise. That's why it's critical for every incumbent to thoroughly analyze and articulate the key elements of its *current* business model before embarking on the process of business model innovation. Again, I cannot overstate this point. While it should be a given that successful companies understand the model that is making them successful, many times this is not the case. We must first peel away the veneer of everyday operations and come to understand the business model at the core of our efforts—how it works, what it enables, and what it inhibits.

BUYING NEW BUSINESS MODELS

Organic new growth is far from a sure bet. New businesses can take years to mature. The skills needed to conceive and incubate them, as we have just seen, present a unique set of challenges that many companies find difficult to overcome. "A large enterprise has trouble making an investment in innovation," says Brad Anderson, the recently retired CEO of electronics retailer Best Buy. "It's in part because Wall Street has trouble imagining a new way to operate but, more important, because people inside the company can't see the value of a new idea and so won't allocate the resources and support the new initiative needs to succeed."[18]

Organic growth is not the only option available to companies seeking transformational growth. Though most of this book has been dedicated to developing new business models within incumbent organizations, that is not meant to imply that incumbents shouldn't seek to achieve transformative growth and exploit opportunities in their white space through acquisition. When Anderson took over Best Buy, he led the company through a series of strategic acquisitions that helped it grow beyond a pure retail sales model.

Some companies are legendary for their acquisitive prowess. For a time, GE acquired dozens of companies a year. Cisco has made more than one hundred acquisitions in its twenty-six year history. Acquisitions can be a way to quickly spur sales and develop reputations. They can allow mature organizations to brand an emerging company as "most likely to succeed" or steadily pursue sound strategic growth. But most of the time, such goals are achieved through sustaining acquisitions bought for their resources and integrated into the parent's existing business model to help fill needed capabilities.

Study after study finds that acquisitions tend to disappoint, variously estimating that half to as many as 80 percent fail to create value.[19] The high-profile struggle of AOL after its $180 billion acquisition of Time Warner is one obvious example of an acquisition gone bad. But there are others: Daimler/Chrysler, Sprint/Nextel, and Quaker Oats/Snapple, to name only a few. Quaker Oats paid $1.7 billion for the Snapple brand in 1994 but sold it to Triarc three years later for a mere $300 million.[20]

By this time, you won't be surprised to learn that I believe many M&A disappointments stem from a failure to understand the fundamentals of business model development. Companies often acquire other companies without fully understanding what they're buying. New resources or products can be folded into the core, but new business models resist. The success of an acquired model frequently lies in its processes and profit formula and very often in the wholly interdependent, integrated nature of its model.

Johnson & Johnson has understood this, buying business models at an early stage and then keeping them separate. For example, its Medical Devices & Diagnostics division bought three business models that were fundamentally new to its respective markets: Vistakon (disposable contact lenses), LifeScan (at-home diabetes monitoring), and Cordis (artery stents used in angioplasty procedures). J&J bought them young and incubated them into the larger enterprise, where they became the growth engine of the MD&D division for many years.

But all too often attempts to fold an acquired business into the core can kill what made it unique in the first place. Video game maker Electronic Arts (EA) learned this the hard way. Propelled by investor expectations, rising development costs, and an industry consolidation trend, EA aggressively bought up small companies

BUSINESS MODEL INNOVATION AS A REPEATABLE PROCESS

FIGURE 35

Growth of J&J's MD&D and consumer divisions

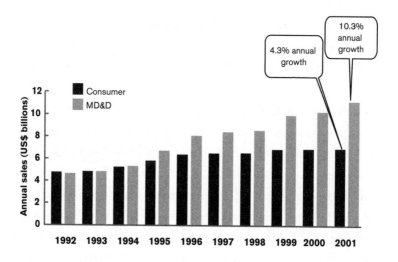

Source: Johnson & Johnson 10-K.

FIGURE 36

Growth from new business models within J&J's MD&D division

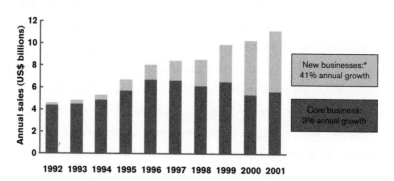

* Includes Cordis starting in 1995.

Source: Johnson & Johnson 10-K.

led by creative teams that had found success in the market. To profit from anticipated economies of scale, it built up a standardized technical infrastructure and imposed streamlined production processes on its new acquisitions.

The results were abysmal. EA fell into a pattern of producing mediocre products based on movie licenses and sports franchises, which were updated each year. "EA is a strong brand, but a predictable one," says Dan Hsu, longtime former editor-in-chief of *Electronic Gaming Monthly*. "Gamers know what they're getting into: something with high production value and solid but not spectacular game play."[21]

Forcing creative teams to follow core processes was killing their innovative spirit. Luckily, CEO John Riccitiello saw the writing on the wall. "Where our industry has made mistake after mistake," he says, "is forcing those technologies down the throats of development teams who know what works . . . It's leading to creative failure . . . We're getting less-creative, less-innovative products."[22]

Then he announced a sea change in EA's operations: independent creative studios would operate as "city-states" within the EA corporate structure. "[Riccitiello] fell on his virtual sword and admitted that his company had squandered its leadership position in the market by trying to reduce the creative process to a cell on a spreadsheet," reported the *New York Times*. "He said his company had lost its way by trying to homogenize and manage its creative process much like the consumer products companies (Häagen-Dazs, PepsiCo, Clorox) he used to work for . . . 'Frankly, the core of our business, like in any creative business, are the guys and women who are actually making the product,' Mr. Riccitiello said. 'You can't just buy people and attempt to apply some business-school synergy to them. It just doesn't work. The companies that succeed are those that provide a stage for their best people and let them do what they do best, and it's taken us some time to understand that. In our business the accountant, the guy in the green eyeshade, is like the guy in the alien movie that eventually gets eaten. If you let him run your business, it is neither inspiring nor effective.'"[23]

Most of the same principles that govern the incubation, acceleration, and transition of homegrown new business models apply to acquired ones as well. Equally important is leadership's ability to allow a newly acquired business model to pull what it needs from the core, rather than having elements of the core model pushed onto it. Best Buy's Brad Anderson expressed this idea succinctly when asked about the company's acquisition of Geek Squad, an in-home computer services and support company. "Geek Squad bought Best Buy," he said, "not the other way around."[24] Anderson knew that the synergy would produce growth and transformation for the company, but he also knew that the low-margin, high-volume, retail mentality of Best Buy could easily suffocate the high-touch, high-margin service orientation of Geek Squad. He let Geek Squad pull from Best Buy what it needed to thrive. At the time of acquisition, Geek Squad had sixty employees and was booking $3 million in annual revenue. Today, working out of seven hundred Best Buy locations across North America, Geek Squad's twelve thousand service agents clock nearly $1 billion in services and return some $280 million to the retailer's bottom line.[25]

As Vijay Govindarajan and Chris Trimble noted in *Ten Rules for Strategic Innovators*, a newly acquired business based on a model distinct from the core should decide what it can borrow from the parent, what it should forget (or forget about), and what it will do or learn that is completely new.[26]

Overcoming Incumbent Challenges

It's the same each time with progress. First they ignore you,
then they say you're mad, then dangerous, then there's a pause
and then you can't find anyone who disagrees with you.

—Tony Benn

Consider a fictional corporation, DogCorp, the world leader in the manufacture of high-quality dogs. Dog-Corp makes great dogs, cutting-edge dogs—the best, most efficient, most innovative dogs in the market. For years, sustaining innovations have allowed DogCorp to post steady growth and earnings, consistent success that has made it the company of choice for talented dog designers and managers throughout the industry. As its pack has grown, DogCorp has built a strong corporate canine culture.

One day, a fairly new manager realizes that, as much as the market loves the pooches DogCorp makes, a significant number of customers need a different kind of pet, a more independent and curious animal, and that need is not being served. Excited by this new market growth opportunity, she puts together a team that designs something new—a cat—to satisfy this unmet need. Then she brings it to her superiors.

And the DogCorp managers go rabid. Pack meetings are called. The financial pit bulls have bones to pick. The poodle managers sit around waiting for some other breed to pet the cat, to signal that the intruder is not dangerous. The hound division stalls; no one there will be promoted for championing a cat, so they just sit and growl. As promising as this cat thing seems to be, something about it doesn't smell right to any of the canine capitalists at DogCorp.

Companies innovate all the time. They innovate products. They innovate marketing efforts. They innovate processes to increase efficiency. Through these efforts, they are innovating and improving their existing business model in an incremental way, streamlining and increasing its efficiency, tweaking the profit formula, bringing new key resources to the table, and changing and refining individual processes. But rarely do incumbent companies make the leap to reinvent their existing business model or create new ones in response to the opportunity or threat presented by a new customer value proposition. Many well-intentioned companies find their innovation efforts thwarted by unknown forces within their organizations. Forward-thinking strategies get hammered into old familiar shapes. Initiatives with promising starts get derailed by powerful constituencies protecting the status quo. Earnest efforts unwittingly render mundane the most exciting new idea.

Why does this keep happening? The business model framework suggests a rational answer. If the core business is successful, it should not be surprising that everyone in the organization is loyal to the model underpinning its success. To learn to be open to the kind of transformative opportunities that require new models, then, we must understand how the existing business model works, through all its many parts, to preserve the status quo, just as it was designed to do.

WHO LET THE DOGS OUT?

There are many ways to skin a cat, the old cliché goes, and just as many ways to kill one. Typically, DogCorp stops nascent kitten ideas before they ever see the light of day. Its managers screen them out from inception, letting only puppies pass through to the marketplace of new ideas. For those kitten ideas that do make it through, the threat of death by dog is far from over; three other dangers lurk. Most commonly, DogCorp will kill off the potential for any cat development through benign neglect, a phenomenon we can call the *non-dog dilemma*. Managers, being smart, recognize the DNA of projects familiar to the corporation's core. A cat lacks the genetic markers identifying it as canine, so when it starts scratching around for something to sustain it, it is not invited into the kennel. It is non-dog, and that is often reason enough for managers to lock the doors. Fundamentally new customer value propositions, ideas that require different profit formulas, or projects that call for different key resources and key processes can all look like non-dogs. If managers could recognize them as cats, they might find potential uses for them or see untapped markets or underserved consumer needs they satisfy. But instead, all thinking stops at the conclusion "non-dog."

Non-dogging manifests itself in companies as a failure to allocate resources, and it can occur up and down the corporate chain of command. Notoriously, Digital Equipment Corporation (DEC), a highly successful manufacturer of minicomputers from the 1960s through the 1980s, looked at the PC—with its substantially different customer, CVP, margin structure, channel to market, and manufacturing requirements—and pronounced it non-dog. CEO Ken Olsen wasn't interested in selling computers piecemeal, having famously said he wanted to own the entire computing structure of his customers' enterprises. DEC actually had a PC under development in its laboratory, eventually sinking $2 billion into the effort, but by the time the poor cat received the serious resource commitment it needed, it was too late.

Similarly, in 1975 Kodak engineer Steve Sasson invented the first digital camera, which captured low-resolution black-and-white images and transferred them to a TV. Perhaps fatally, he dubbed it "filmless photography" when he demonstrated the device for various leaders at the company. "After taking a few pictures of the attendees at the meeting and displaying them on the TV set in the room," says Sasson, "the questions started coming. Why would anyone ever want to view his or her pictures on a TV? How would you store these images? What does an electronic photo album look like?"[1] Later Sasson recalled management's overall assessment of the development. "It was filmless photography," he said, "so management's reaction was, 'that's cute—but don't tell anyone about it.'"[2] Kodak non-dogged it. Though Kodak's research labs had produced brilliant technologies, the products languished. "It seems Kodak had developed antibodies against anything that might compete with film," says Bill Lloyd, Kodak's recently retired chief technical officer.[3] It took more than twenty-five years for Kodak to find success in the digital camera market with its Easyshare brand.

The second danger is the organizational urge to cram new opportunities into the existing business model. Let's call that *dogging the cat*. "Your new cat venture calls for furry mice to fulfill its play needs," says the well-intentioned Product Happiness Manager, "but we have a state-of-the-art stick supply chain and an advanced throwing system we believe will be more economical." And it is more economical. But the cats couldn't care less.

Unhappy, they don't purr or pounce. Instead they grow neurotic and start scratching the furniture. No one wants to buy a crazy cat, so the whole idea is scrapped. Or, if it does make it to the market, the cat-that-fetches is such a strange animal no one buys it. It matches no one's job-to-be done.

Dogging the cat can also be viewed as the business version of a political legislative process. An observant manager sees an unmet need in a market and writes a nifty customer value proposition describing how to meet that need. The new CVP enters the system, and the influential design group hears about it. That group lends its support but introduces a small change to keep it within existing design paradigms. Then the marketing organization gets on board—with a few changes to make it more appealing to the existing customer base. And the powerful finance group revises the pricing, margins, and cost basis to conform to "what makes us great." And on it goes. To gain the support of the many people who must vote to ratify the bill, it gets amended, weakened, and sometimes changed beyond recognition until everyone's best intentions end up creating a Frankenstein's monster: a product or service that serves no one's needs at all.

As originally conceived, for example, the U.S. Army's Bradley Fighting Vehicle was to be a light, fast, armored personnel carrier capable of getting a dozen or so troops into and out of a theater of operations quickly and safely. That was before a succession of Pentagon generals, inculcated with the military's core model predisposition for highly complex systems, dogged it into a combination troop carrier/scout vehicle/antitank weapon platform. To accommodate its tank-killing weaponry, troop capacity was reduced to six. To reach scouting speed, its hull was made of lightweight, vulnerable aluminum.[4] Seventeen years of development and $13 billion later, those conflicting specifications produced "a troop transport that can't carry troops, a reconnaissance vehicle that's too conspicuous to do reconnaissance, and a quasi-tank that has less armor than a snow blower but carries enough ammo to take out half of D.C."[5] A live-fire test finally exposed its weaknesses; a single shell annihilated it.

Even within a highly innovative culture like Hilti's, the temptation to dog the cat is almost irresistible. "In a fleet process, you define the spot in the life cycle of a tool when it should be replaced, and we were refreshing tools before they broke down," explains Hilti sales and marketing head Marco Meyrat. "Our business unit, whose habitual thinking was to extract maximum value from our investments, suggested that we extend the life of the tool in the fleet. But this very natural thought jeopardized the value proposition of the fleet management program. If our customers were not getting the latest technology and their tools were breaking down more frequently, they would begin to wonder whether they were getting good value from the contract."[6]

Finally, assaults on nascent initiatives can be less subtle. Sometimes, someone just wants to outright *attack the cat*. As the core organization struggles to meet its numbers or address a major operational problem or growth opportunity that needs more resources, these projects can face sudden death. Entrenched departments often worry about cannibalization; they fear that the new cat could become a dog-eating tiger, consuming critical resources and endangering the entire kennel. Or if the core organization runs out of patience and expects the new venture to grow at the pace and on the scale of the traditional core-growth initiatives, the venture can be shut down or brought back into the mainstream organization to face a slower but just as certain death.

This is precisely what happened to a project aptly named Kittyhawk at Hewlett-Packard in the early 1990s. Part of HP's disk memory division, the Kittyhawk team embarked on a disruptive play with a 1.3-inch hard disk drive, a cat that was a far cry from even the smallest 3.5-inch dog in HP's pack. It was meant to be a "small, dumb, cheap" disk drive that could power diminutive devices like the Nintendo Game Boy and PDAs for UPS drivers, a whole new market. But the disk memory division was very impatient for growth: it had its sights set on the big dogs at IBM and Seagate and wanted to bulk up quickly. So it projected second-year revenue growth at $100 million, a highly ambitious number. This did not give the Kittyhawk team the time it needed to explore the Nintendo opportunities and other promising propositions as they came along. Having been set up to fail, Kittyhawk did so, and the project was shut down by 1994, just over two years after its initial launch.[7]

THE PROBLEM OF THE EXISTING RULES, NORMS, AND METRICS

The DogCorp metaphor is a lighthearted way to illustrate the things people do in the service of their existing business model. These impulses are often implicit, arising not as direct imperatives of the model but in response to the business rules, behavioral norms, and related success metrics that have developed to allow the model to be executed effectively, repeatedly, and efficiently. These invisible guardians of the prevailing business model are essential for managing and executing operations and innovation efforts focused on growing the core or pursuing adjacencies. But they are poison to new business models. They are the essence of dog.

The established norms of a business can limit how far a project team will venture from traditional offerings, precluding new approaches to what can be sold (like moving from a product to a service) or how an offering can be sold (like moving from physical stores to the Internet—or vice versa). When fundamentally new CVPs are devised, established rules can prevent the changes in the profit formula or in key resources and processes needed to make it thrive.

FIGURE 37

Common rules of thumb derived from the core business model that interfere with the requirements of the new business model

Financial	Operational	Marketing/Sales/R&D/HR
Gross margins	End-product quality	Pricing
Opportunity size	Supplier quality	Performance demands
Unit pricing	Owned vs. outsourced manufacturing	Product-development life cycles
Unit margin	Customer service level	Basis for individuals' rewards and incentives
Time to break even	Channel options	Brand parameters
Net present value calculations	Lead times	
Credit terms	Throughput	

The Locked Nature of the Profit Formula

Those financial pit bulls? They are merely acting to protect the company's current profit formula. Expected margins of the core enterprise, for example, can lead them to reject out of hand the possibility of a business model innovation built around a different margin model, even if the other parts of the profit formula could be changed to describe a potentially profitable white-space play—say, by coupling lower margins with lower overhead, lower cost structure, and higher resource velocity. The rigidity inherent in the existing cost structure, especially when it comes to overhead, together with the challenges involved in making structural changes to the resource velocity of the business, make it difficult for a business unit to accept initiatives that require new unit margin targets.

When Marco Meyrat brought the new fleet management service to his financial analysts at Hilti, he encountered just this sort of subtle resistance. "Our finance people thought there was too much unknown risk of tool loss and repair costs," he says, "so they took a—how shall I say—*very safe* view toward pricing. I had to work to keep it affordable. If you price a new offering too high, you kill it before it starts."[8] When Hilti expanded the model to markets outside Switzerland, the finance team again tried to increase pricing without regard for the overall value of the CVP. Again, Meyrat struggled not only to maintain the integrity of the business model innovation but also to prove its value to Finance. "There are always *yes but*–ers," he says, "who find a reason to say *but.*"

Don Sheets at Dow Corning encountered similar problems in the incubation of Xiameter. Finance shot down his early profit formula because it called for smaller margins than Dow Corning's core high-touch sales and solution business. It wasn't until he developed a model that maintained something close to those high margins and dramatically lowered costs to achieve the reduced target price point that he won the department's support. It was an end-around run that luckily succeeded, but the showdown just as easily could have stopped the project in its tracks.

The financial officers in these examples did not take unreasonable positions; they were just unable to conceive of new profit formulas. One error I frequently encounter when considering new growth opportunities is something Clay Christensen calls the *doctrine of marginal costs.*[9] Faced with a new business proposition requiring a new business model that includes capital investment in new capabilities or infrastructure, finance people will commonly respond, "Why would we build this new thing when the marginal cost of utilizing our existing capacity is half or a third of that? Why build a new machine when the existing machine still has some more room to do stuff?" They are looking at the minimal variable costs of producing new products using an existing machine, but they fail to consider the large, already amortized investment in it. So creating a new product from a new machine seems very expensive because they must factor in the investment in capital and associated new capabilities. The marginal cost comparison is accurate on its face, but comparing the costs of the new model to the possible profits of extending the old one is comparing apples to grapes. The conclusion that it should necessarily cost less to use the existing sales force to sell a lower-margin product than to train a whole new one arises from the same sort of mistaken reasoning.

This financial analysis is even more destructive when it fails to consider the possibility that the new idea has the potential to disrupt and replace the old profit formula entirely. Big Steel companies failed to accurately assess the more profitable business model of the electric arc-furnace mini-mills, which went on to ultimately decimate their business. By ignoring the sunk costs of existing infrastructure when calculating the returns from marginal growth— and not accounting for the potential disruptive costs of doing nothing—you get incorrect numbers that stop dead the possibility of something new.

The Illogic of Leveraging Core Capabilities

The existing key resources and processes that underpin the core model can exert a profound influence on managers who daily keep the enterprise going. They often try to leverage core capabilities whether or not these serve the new model. Sony engineers had a cultural aversion to hard-drive technology, for example, which they found inelegant, so they were reluctant to pursue the MP3 space. Kodak initially ran from filmless imaging. Of course, white-space plays don't exclude exploiting existing capabilities— the iPod itself is a hardware/software integration product, right in

Apple's wheelhouse—but new business models must be free to borrow what they need from the core and reinvent the rest.

The rules of an established model are particularly toxic to a new one because they frequently look like sound business reasons to avoid the unknown. It can be hard to recognize how they impede new growth, and even those most aware of their influence can unwittingly fall prey to their restrictive effect. A few years back, I worked with a newly acquired company that its parent understood had a different business model requiring a different way of operating. Although it was supposed to be kept separate from the parent, it still had to adhere to 150 business rules and related metrics—all of which kept the acquired company's CEO traveling more to internal meetings than to visits with customers.

REDEFINING THE RULES

No man can serve two masters, the saying goes, and when a company ventures into its white space with a new business model that carries a different set of rules and metrics from those of the core, it's critical that everyone be clear about which set of rules they should be following. Otherwise they will face an impossible conflict of interest. Worse, different people will resolve this conflict differently, which will undermine the organization in unpredictable ways.

Middle managers working on a new business innovation project who have not been explicitly released from the rules governing the core business model rarely feel it is in their best interests—or the best interests of their organizations—to embrace the new business model. It's not that they are inherently antagonistic to the new thing; it's that they don't feel they've been discharged from their responsibility to the old thing. Business-unit heads who are charged with carrying out the core business and delivering on budgets within the allotted time may find it difficult to know how to simultaneously meet the requirements of the different budget and operations of a new initiative.

What's more, while it may be clear that an innovation project carries different expectations about profitability and growth than the core does, people's compensation packages, promotions, bonuses, and recognition are often tied not to any project, new or old, but to the near-term success of the broader company. While this might be perfectly reasonable for those parts of the organization aimed at sustaining incremental growth, near-term incentives are counterproductive to new business development that might take years to reach fruition. Business model innovations are inherently uncertain, it's hard to predict how long they'll take to generate substantial revenue streams, and they are more prone to failure than innovation moves within the core. Who can blame a rational up-and-comer for thinking: "If I do something inconsistent with the way I'm measured, I'll miss my marks"?

Unfortunately, companies rarely allow for more than one career path within a function. Nor do they allow two sets of reward systems to co-exist within the corporation, let alone within a business unit. Inhibitors to innovation like these are deep-seated and are almost never exposed to the light of day, a tendency identified by leadership expert Steven Kerr in his classic essay "On the Folly of Rewarding A, While Hoping for B."[10]

The types of innovation-killing and change-phobic behaviors described in this chapter are often blamed on lower-level employees. Explicitly delineating the two sets of rules that the two business models require can resolve a lot of unnecessary conflict and risk-avoidance behavior on their part. The rules governing the core business model are necessary. And workers honor them, as they should. They should keep on doing so until senior executives explicitly replace them with a new business model, built on a customer value proposition and profit formula so different that they require new processes and resources and, in turn, new rules.

ADDRESSING CHALLENGES AT THE TOP

For the sake of simplicity, I've been talking all along about business model innovation as it would occur in the simplest of companies—that is, in an organization with only one offering attached to only one business model. But of course many, many companies operate as corporations with more than one business unit, each having a uniquely honed business model. In this sense, a corporation does not have a business model; it is a collection of business models. In my observation, it's nearly impossible for a business unit to adopt and operate more than one business model at a time and do them all well. So, essentially when a business unit's model has run its course, not only the business model but the business unit itself dies off. The life of the corporation continues, but it is carried on in the other ongoing business units and through the creation of new business units with new business models. It is by creating, operating, trading, and closing business units (and their associated business models) that corporations stay vibrant, continue to grow, and remain relevant to customers who have real, important, and changing jobs to get done.[11]

It is in this context that the challenges of business model innovation should be viewed at the corporate executive level. Like their business-unit counterparts, top leaders must learn to recognize and overcome the influence of existing core business models in the pursuit of their company's white space. Upper management is paid to grow the corporation. It's also charged with managing risk. For many, white-space pursuits appear overly risky because they lie outside the core or close adjacencies of any of their business units. Past failure from directionless stabs into the white space can become permanently lodged in institutional memory. "We've tried this before and it didn't work," says the once-burnt executive, unable to see that the previous failure was caused by the absence of a structured approach. The odds of success are greatly increased if executives understand how the imperatives of the new model differ from those of the existing one.

Cannibalization concerns may be heightened for leaders, who make the ultimate decisions about new initiatives. To support a project that at first blush seems to risk existing business and current customers requires an unusual mind-set, one that thoroughly understands how all four boxes in the business model framework work. Creating a new model for a new job does not mean the current model is threatened or should be changed. A new model can reinforce and complement the core business, as Dow Corning discovered.

Leaders, too, are often uncomfortable not knowing how quickly a white-space opportunity will reach its full potential. A predisposition for bamboo-fast opportunities can make oak tree seedlings seem insignificant and unworthy of further support. New models should be profitable early on but will likely not yield high revenue until their scale accelerates. Leadership teams habituated to managing for the short term can easily become impatient for growth, killing young projects with long-term potential in search of faster returns.

When leaders are uncomfortable pursuing something new, how can they ever expect anyone else in the company to do so? To seize the white space, leaders must learn to balance the company's investment in sustaining growth with direct investment in new value propositions that require new business models. They must authorize the formation of teams capable of creating these models and then protect and nurture them. Such teams should not be large, but they do have to be focused mainly on the new venture. Members shouldn't be asked to split their time between core and new growth efforts. And the teams need the freedom to establish their own business rhythm—not be forced to conform to the prevailing way things are done. Innovation teams must have the authority to relax the rules of the core and then develop new rules and metrics that support the new CVP. That authority can only come from the top.

STRATEGY AND BUSINESS MODELS

Harvard Business School historian Alfred Chandler famously argued that "structure follows strategy."[12] And many senior managers believe that the business structure needed to achieve a new strategy will somehow naturally evolve. They are frequently disappointed. As we now understand, the structure that executes a strategy is governed by the imperatives of its business model. In reality, strategy follows from structure in the typical strategic-planning process.

Most companies develop their corporate strategy in a deliberate, annual operational exercise that focuses on incrementally improving the core. Strategic initiatives arising from core-based assumptions, however, most often return core-based strategies, and this is what is fundamentally broken about most strategic-planning efforts. Within the context of an operational exercise, the capabilities of the core business model limit what strategies can be considered.

Rather than employ a mechanistic *strategic-planning* process, organizations looking to grow in new ways should create a *strategy development* process. To open up their organizations to transformational possibilities, leaders must stop peering through the lens of their traditional CVP, their established profit formula, and their current combination of resources and processes and truly embrace Chandler's prescription.[13]

For structure to follow strategy, the strategy development team must begin with the root of how value is created—the customer. It must identify, or at least be aware of, the critical unsatisfied jobs of current and potential customers before deciding how best to achieve the company's growth objectives. The team should then consider how to pursue those objectives with a set of real options, one or more of which completely reimagines the business model required to change the game within its industry, transform existing markets, or create new ones.

The leadership team should then converge on the appropriate strategy, articulating the types of innovation projects suitable for project teams to tackle. In this way, white-space initiatives are melded with overall corporate strategy. Strategy development must remain a flexible, creative process; leaders must make a conscious effort to keep the rules and norms of the core in abeyance while they allow their strategy team to imagine new growth and renewal through business model innovations.

Leadership ultimately answers to a broad assortment of stakeholders, including board members, analysts, and investors. Many become gun-shy when faced with investors impatient for growth and wary of new business initiatives that stray too far from the core. "Every new business we've ever engaged in has initially been seen as a distraction by people externally, and sometimes even internally," says Amazon CEO Jeff Bezos. "They'll say, 'Why are you expanding outside of media products? Why are you going international? Why are you entering the marketplace business with third-party sellers?' These are fair questions. But they all have at their heart one of the reasons that it's so difficult for incumbent companies to pursue new initiatives. It's because even if they are wild successes, they usually have no meaningful impact on the company's economics for years."[14]

These questions arise because companies large and small have often failed in the past, leaving investors and analysts skittish. The Street prefers safe, stick-to-your-knitting strategies. Unfortunately, even when executives spot a fantastic growth opportunity in their white space, they often don't know how to articulate the new value proposition and how the organization will fundamentally change to support it. They are stymied in their attempts to justify a set of financials so foreign to the norm. So the analysts penalize the company with a negative report. It needn't be so. Using the business model framework, leaders could make their plans for seizing transformational growth opportunities less of a mystery to stakeholders of all kinds. The goal would not be just to set expectations about the prospects for new initiatives but to set them into the larger corporate context.

With that in mind, you could start, as I did with this book, by explaining to stakeholders the problem of the growth gap— that is, the reason your company needs to move past the core and adjacencies, why remaining too close to home is actually a greater risk than a well-managed trip into your white space. Then you need to explicate a corporate strategy that includes how you plan to continue your existing CVP growth while embarking on new growth, specifying how much you plan to invest in business model innovation. At this point you are not advocating one course of action or another. You should be open to all sorts of alternatives to your current models. If you are open, so too will your company be to thinking of a portfolio of truly breakthrough customer value propositions.

The dogs guarding the gates of innovation are many and varied, and they often lurk there in disguise. Launching and managing an organization on the path to transformational growth or renewal in the white space requires keeping a vigilant watch for their presence. Leaders who embrace and communicate the necessity of business model innovation are the ones who will make it safely past the gates and into the profitable white space.

Epilogue

The world is moving so fast nowadays that the man who says
it can't be done is generally interrupted by someone doing it.

—attributed to Elbert Hubbard

Peter Drucker once said, "Every organization . . . has a theory of the business . . . Some theories of the business are so powerful that they last for a long time. But . . . they don't last forever, and, indeed, today they rarely last for very long at all. Eventually every theory of the business becomes obsolete and then invalid."[1] The average life span of those theories grows shorter every day. Building a great business and operating it well no longer guarantees you'll be around in 100 years, or even 20. In 1958, the average length of time a company remained on the S&P 500 was 57 years; by 1983, it had dropped to 30 years; in 2008, it was just 18.[2]

I believe investing for the long term in the twenty-first century means continually building and rebuilding your organization. Shorter business life cycles require a new sort of management discipline capable of leading an organization through an ongoing process of transformation and renewal. To thrive in today's marketplace, to be built to last, every business now must be built to *transform*.

A lot has been written about Internet pioneer Amazon as it emerged from the dot-com bubble as one of the few winners and continued to blaze a trail of impressive growth (from about $4 billion in 2002 to nearly $20 billion in 2008). But one of the most unexamined facets of its high-profile success is its unabashed embrace of transformational growth in its white space.[3] Amazon survived the dot-com bust initially because, unlike many of its contemporaries, it had a viable and innovative business model built around a market-changing customer value proposition and a radical profit formula, which upended the staid book industry. Then it quickly expanded beyond books to include all sorts of easily shippable consumer goods, growing from its core into near adjacencies. But Amazon didn't stop there.

A few years later, the company seized its white space when it devised a new value proposition, offering a commission-based brokerage service to buyers and sellers of used books. Then it moved into its white space again by developing a model to serve an entirely different customer: third-party sellers. By opening up its storefront to other retailers that were essentially competitors, Amazon transformed its business from direct sales to a sales-and-service model, aggregating many sellers under one virtual roof and receiving commissions from the other companies' sales.

Then Amazon did it yet again. After it expanded its IT resources in early 2000, it identified a new area of potential growth by finding another new customer—the IT community. Serving this new customer's needs required different processes, different resources, and a different profit formula—in short, another new business model. In 2002, after a careful period of incubation, Amazon launched a Web services platform that offered low-cost, reliable, and easy-to-use online services for other Web sites, as well as client-side applications for Web developers.[4] It may have seemed risky for a young company that had only reached profitability in that same year to invest its innovation resources in new business models rather than stick to its core, but within five years the site used by those services had grown into the seventh-largest in the world.[5]

And Amazon kept going. In late 2007, it hired palmOne's former VP of hardware engineering Gregg Zehr and set up Lab126. Its first product, the Kindle e-book reader, came to market wrapped in a business model not only foreign to Amazon's DNA but also potentially disruptive to the entire publishing industry. To launch a high-margin, product-based offering, Amazon had to become an original equipment manufacturer (OEM). It wrapped this technology in a seamlessly integrated iTunes-type digital media platform that combined both transaction-based content delivery and a subscription model for periodical content. It partnered with content producers in new and innovative ways and created an open back-end that allowed independent publishers to generate new content specifically for the Kindle platform. In its first year, Kindle sold an estimated 500,000 units and earned high customer satisfaction ratings.[6] Amazon has greatly expanded the market for e-books and has positioned itself for success not only in this now suddenly viable market but in newspaper and periodical distribution as well.

Amazon at its roots is built to transform. When it finds opportunities to serve new customers, or existing customers in new ways, it conceives and builds new business models to exploit them. Amazon has the unique ability to create and operate at the same time—to invest for the long term by launching and running entirely new types of businesses while simultaneously extracting value from existing businesses. It demonstrates that *becoming* can become a part of *being* for any organization willing to invest the time, discipline, and effort. Whatever its future holds, Amazon's journey will likely be marked by a series of transformations, as it continues to pursue its vision unafraid of white space, business model innovation, or renewal.

To be built to transform requires the courage to focus on delivering value for the customer first. Identifying value begins by thinking of an important unserved or underserved job that customers want done and then coming up with a well-defined value proposition to address that job, however foreign to your current offerings that may be. "If you want to continuously revitalize the service that you offer to your customers, you cannot stop at what you are good at," says CEO Jeff Bezos. "You have to ask what your customers need and want, and then, no matter how hard it is, you better get good at those things."[7] With a well-defined customer value proposition serving a focused, well-articulated job, business leaders and project teams can work together to design the appropriate profit formulas, key resources, and key processes the company needs to thrive.

To do this, business leaders need to become business model thinkers, to understand that both the current model underpinning their existing business and any new models they may devise are complex systems with interdependent elements that must work together to deliver real value. To build these systems, they must think like architects or engineers, to begin with blueprints, build prototypes, and develop working structures that can deliver on new areas of opportunity. Although they can't devise all the answers up front, they can ask the right questions. Then they must pursue those answers like an artist would, exploring with a process of structured creativity that allows everyone involved to freely imagine the possible, not just the easily done.

Business model innovation efforts should be focused on the pursuit of something grand—changing the game in an existing market, creating a whole new market, transforming an entire industry. If leaders can't succinctly articulate how a new business model will capture an opportunity for significant corporate growth (or in the face of tectonic shifts become a powerful engine of company renewal), then white-space efforts or fundamental business model change is unjustified. Business model innovators should be hunters of big game and leave the harvesting of core assets to others.

But while thinking big is an essential precondition for seizing the white space, it is equally imperative to start small. Slowly incubating the new venture using foothold markets will protect it as it grows and matures, giving it the time and space needed to test assumptions, make adjustments, and develop the key resources and processes that will deliver the greatest value.

Ultimately, companies need to learn how to get out of their own way. To many, this will seem like the hardest challenge, but I believe that much of the frustration leaders, managers, and employees encounter in trying to do something new stems from an insufficient understanding of the old. Too many companies don't actually know what business models they're currently operating under, going along day to day using rules of thumb, incentives, and the odd success story to guide them. But organizations that have an explicit understanding of the elements that make up their current business models are in a far better position to judge how well equipped they are to capitalize on new opportunities or meet coming threats.

Business model innovation thrives in cultures of inquiry, environments in which new value propositions and ideas for new business models are met with interest and encouragement. In built-to-transform companies, managers recognize that a nascent business opportunity, no matter how non-dog it is, might be the key to the Next Big Thing. "Controlling innovation is an oxymoron," says Netflix CEO Reed Hastings. "You inspire innovation. You support innovation. Unlike the quality process, where the goal is to reduce variability, innovations require you to look for ways to increase variability. And business model innovation is scary because it is the toughest to take on."[8]

It doesn't have to be. Throughout this book, I have detailed a structured approach to the essentially unstructured process of creating something new. I have shown that while forays into your white space carry a high degree of uncertainty, they needn't carry a high level of risk. An organization can make business model innovation a management discipline—a repeatable process that can be well understood.

Seizing your white space begins with a simple four-box business model framework, but it leads to far-reaching implications for all organizations navigating the turbulent waters of twenty-first-century global business. Business model innovation can help companies meet many of the big challenges they face, be they growth gaps, market shifts, revolutionary technologies, or uncontrollable social forces. It can help companies devise profitable, market-based solutions to the needs of consumers and societies around the world that will make people's lives better and economies more prosperous. To create new growth, spur transformational change, and renew our companies, we must learn to seize the white space through business model innovation.

NOTES

Chapter 1

1. "Lockheed-Martin 'Skunk Works' P791," http://www.youtube.com/watch?v=W3n5cUaG5fg.

2. "Hovercraft in Military Operations," *HoverWorld Insider*, March 2006, http://www.worldhovercraft.org/insider/mar06.htm#military/.

3. David E. Rosenbaum, "Arms Makers and Military Face a Wrenching New Era," *New York Times*, August 4, 1991, http://query.nytimes.com/gst/fullpage.html?res=9D0CE0DE1F38F937A3575BC0A967958260&sec=&spon=&pagewanted=4/.

4. Clayton M. Christensen and Michael E. Raynor, *The Innovator's Solution: Creating and Sustaining Successful Growth* (Boston: Harvard Business School Press, 2003), chapter 9.

5. Chris Zook and James Allen, *Profit From the Core: Growth Strategy in an Era of Turbulence* (Boston: Harvard Business School Press, 2001); also Chris Zook, *Beyond the Core: Expand Your Market Without Abandoning Your Roots* (Boston: Harvard Business School Press, 2004); and Chris Zook, *Unstoppable: Finding Hidden Assets to Renew the Core and Fuel Profitable Growth* (Boston: Harvard Business School Press, 2007).

6. Owen W. Linzmayer, *Apple Confidential 2.0: The Definitive History of the World's Most Colorful Company*, 2nd ed. (San Francisco: No Starch Press, 2004), 68; and "Dangerous Limbo at Apple," *BusinessWeek*, July 21, 1997.

7. Mikael Hagén, "Best Data's Cabo," http://www.3dss.com/reviews/Cabo/Cabo.html/.

8. In fact, iTunes music may be a loss leader for the company. Of the $0.99 Apple collected per song, about two-thirds went to the music label and another 22 percent went to credit card processing, leaving Apple about a dime to cover the cost of the site and other direct and indirect costs (noted in David B. Yoffie and Michael Slind, "Apple Computer, 2006," Case 9-706-496 [Boston: Harvard Business School Publishing, 2007], 14).

9. "Apple's iTunes and iPod," May 28, 2009, data gathered by the author from an aggregate of sources including internal Innosight research, Apple 10k 2003–2008, and Yahoo Finance.

10. Randy Stross, "How the iPod Ran Circles Around the Walkman," *New York Times*, March 13, 2005.

11. "Business Model Innovation in U.S. Retailing and Airline Industries," May 28, 2009, data gathered by the author from an aggregate of sources including internal Innosight research and Datastream.

12. "Business Model Innovators Founded in Last Quarter Century That Have Entered *Fortune* 500 in Last Decade," May 28, 2009, data gathered by the author from an aggregate of sources including internal Innosight research, Reuters, and Google Finance.

13. IBM Global CEO Study, "The Enterprise of the Future," 2008.

14. "The Quest for Innovation: A Global Study of Innovation Management 2006–2016," American Management Association (2006), 74.

Chapter 2

1. Adapted from Konstantin Stanislavsky and Elizabeth Reynolds Hapgood, *An Actor Prepares* (1936; reprinted New York: Taylor & Francis, 1989), 177–181.

2. Peter Drucker, "The Theory of the Business," *Harvard Business Review*, September–October 1994, 95–104.

3. Joan Magretta, *What Management Is: How It Works, and Why It's Everyone's Business* (New York: Free Press, 2002), 46.

4. For example, Henry William Chesbrough, *Open Business Models: How to Thrive in the New Innovation Landscape* (Boston: Harvard Business School Press, 2006); and Henry William Chesbrough, *Open Innovation: The New Imperative for Creating and Profiting from Technology* (Boston: Harvard Business School Press, 2003).

5. Key resources and processes can also be termed *company capabilities* or, organized in a certain way, can be used to describe the value chain of a business.

6. The term *jobs-to-be-done* was coined by Gage Foods CEO Richard Pedi, and the concept has been greatly extended by Clay

Christensen. See, for instance, Clayton Christensen and Michael E. Raynor, *The Innovator's Solution: Creating and Sustaining Successful Growth* (Boston: Harvard Business School Press, 2003), chapter 3.

7. Theodore Levitt, "Marketing Myopia," *Harvard Business Review* (Best of HBR 1960), July 2004, 1–13.

8. Clayton M. Christensen and Michael E. Raynor, *The Innovator's Solution: Creating and Sustaining Successful Growth* (Boston: Harvard Business School Press, 2003), 99, footnote 17.

9. Of course, now many people have removed their land lines and rely solely on their cell phones.

10. Peter Drucker, *Managing for Results* (New York: Collins, 1993), 94.

11. Charles D. Ellis, Anne M. Mulcahy, and Joel M. Podolny, *Joe Wilson and the Creation of Xerox* (Hoboken, NJ: John Wiley & Sons, 2006), 196.

12. There are cases when high prices create value for customers (exclusive residential enclaves, golf course memberships, and art masterpieces come to mind), but these are far from common.

13. Krishna G. Palepu and Vishnu Srinivasan, "Tata Motors: The Tata Ace," Case 9-108-011(Boston: Harvard Business Publishing, 2008), 15.

14. Vipin V. Nair, "Tata Motors Gets 203,000 Orders for Nano, World's Cheapest Car," *Bloomberg*, May 4, 2009; and Stuart Burns, "Tata Nano's Sales Show the Way Forward for Detroit?" http://agmetalminer.com/2009/05/12/tatas-nano-sales-show-the-way-forward-for-detroit/.

15. Nancy F. Koehn and Katherine Miller, "John Mackey and Whole Foods Market," Case 9-807-111 (Boston: Harvard Business School Publishing, 2007), 9.

16. Clayton Christensen and Richard S. Tedlow, "Patterns of Disruption in Retailing," *Harvard Business Review*, January–February 2000, 42–45.

17. Ronald Fink, "Forget the Float? The 2001 Working Capital Survey," *CFO Magazine*, July 1, 2001, http://www.cfo.com/article.cfm/2997693/.

18. William A. Sahlman and Laurence E. Katz, "Amazon.com—Going Public," Case 9-899-003 (Boston: Harvard Business School Publishing, 1998), 22.

19. Phillip Elmer-DeWitt, "How to Grow the iPod as the MP3 Player Market Shrinks," *CNN Money*, January 29, 2008, http://apple20.blogs.

fortune.cnn.com/2008/01/29/beyond-the-incredible-shrinking-ipod-market/.

20. "iTunes 'Biggest US Music Seller,'" *BBC News*, April 4, 2004, http://news.bbc.co.uk/2/hi/business/7329886.stm.

21. As of this writing, it's still unclear whether Tata's Nano will achieve initial profitability with this profit formula.

22. John R. Wells and Travis Haglock, "Whole Foods Market, Inc.," Case 9-705-476 (Boston: Harvard Business School Publishing, 2005), 5–6.

23. Koehn and Miller, "John Mackey and Whole Foods Market," 8.

24. Thomas L. Friedman, *The World Is Flat* (New York: Picador, 2007), 167.

25. Thomas M. Box and Kent Byus, "Ryanair (2005): Successful Low Cost Leadership," *Proceedings from the International Academy for Case Studies* 12, no. 2 (2005), 10–11.

26. "Tata Nano Is a Unique Case Study of OEM-Supplier Partnership," SupplierBusiness.com newsletter, January 14, 2008, http://www.autoindustry.co.uk/news/15-01-08_6/.

27. Wells and Haglock, "Whole Foods Market, Inc.," 8.

28. "Company History," http://www.wholefoodsmarket.com/company/history.php; and Samuel Sen, "Whole Foods Market—To Be or B2B" (Austin, TX: McCombs School of Business, Fall 2001), 1.

Chapter 3

1. "Highlights from the History of Dow Corning Corporation, the Silicone Pioneer," Dow Corning Corporation, Form No. 01-4027-01, 2007.

2. C. K. Prahalad and M. S. Krishnan, *The New Age of Innovation: Driving Co-Created Value Through Global Networks* (New York: McGraw-Hill, 2008), 199.

3. David J. Morrow, "Statement on Breast Implant Claims," *New York Times*, November 10, 1998.

4. The discussion of Dow Corning in this chapter comes from an interview by the author on November 1, 2006, with Don Sheets, corporate vice president and chief financial officer of Dow Corning.

5. Clayton M. Christensen, *The Innovator's Dilemma: When New Technologies Cause Great Firms to Fail* (Boston: Harvard Business School Press, 1997), 183; and Geoffrey A. Moore, *Crossing the Chasm* (New York: HarperBusiness, 1991). Companies can compete and differentiate on more than one level of performance. For the purpose of this conversation, I am focused on the *primary* basis of competition.

6. Stephen E. Lin and Enrico Senger, "Case Study Xiameter—E-Commerce Solution Covering Business Customer Ordering and Information Processes," Center for Digital Strategies at Tuck School of Business at Dartmouth (Hanover, NH), and Institute of Information Management, University of St. Gallen (St. Gallen, Switzerland), 2003.

7. Ron Fillmore, Global Executive Director of Xiameter, interview by author, tape recording from phone interview, October 18, 2006.

8. The discussion of Hilti in this chapter comes from an interview by the author on June 17, 2008, with Marco Meyrat, member of the executive board and head of worldwide sales and marketing at Hilti.

9. Pius Baschera, interview by author, tape recording from phone interview, June 3, 2008.

10. "Fred Smith on the Birth of FedEx," The Great Innovators/Online Extra, *BusinessWeek*, September 20, 2004, http://www.businessweek.com/magazine/content/04_38/b3900032_mz072.htm.

11. Amar V. Bhidé, *The Origin and Evolution of New Business* (Oxford: Oxford University Press, 2000), 185.

Chapter 4

1. Rekhu Balu, "Strategic Innovation: Hindustan Lever Ltd.," *Fast Company*, May 2001.

2. "Hindustan Unilever," June 10, 2009, data gathered by the author from "Income Statements" and "Ratios and Returns" from http://finapps.forbes.com.

3. Nitin Paranjpe, interview by author, tape recording from phone interview, July 11, 2008.

4. V. Kasturi Rangan and Rohithari Rajan, "Unilever in India: Hindustan Lever's Project Shakti—Marketing FMCG to the Rural Consumer," Case 9-505-056 (Boston: Harvard Business School, 2002), 6; and 2001 Census of India.

5. Paranjpe, interview.

6. Scott Anthony, Mark W. Johnson, Joseph V. Sinfield, and Elizabeth J. Altman, *The Innovator's Guide to Growth: Putting Disruptive Innovation to Work* (Boston: Harvard Business Press, 2008), 48–59.

7. Ming Zen and Peter J. Williamson, "The Hidden Dragons," in *Harvard Business Review on Doing Business in China*, ed. Kenneth Lieberthal (Boston: Harvard Business School Press, 2004), 68.

8. Justin Lahart, Patrick Barta, and Andrew Batson, "New Limits to Grow Revive Malthusian Fears," *Wall Street Journal*, March 24, 2008.

9. Govind Rajan, interview by author, tape recording from phone interview, June 27, 2008.

10. Ibid.

11. Ibid.

12. Paranjpe, interview.

13. As the initiative later achieved scale and market acceptance, margin levels increased.

14. Paranjpe, interview; and "The Micro Business with Massive Impact," *Impact on Global Issues*, 24, http://www.unilever.com/images/ProjectShakti-microBusMassImpact_tcm13-118538.pdf.

15. Krishnendu Dasgupta, interview by author, tape recording from phone interview, July 2, 2008.

16. Sanjiv Kakkar, interview by author, tape recording from phone interview, June 24, 2008.

17. Chris Trimble, "Hindustan Lever," Case 2-0011 (Hanover, NH: Tuck School of Business at Dartmouth, 2002).

18. Kakkar, interview.

19. Dasgupta, interview.

20. "Marketing to Rural India: Making the Ends Meet," *India Knowledge @ Wharton* (2007), 2–3; and Rangan and Rajan, "Unilever in India."

21. Dasgupta, interview.

22. Paranjpe, interview.

23. Ibid.

24. "India: Creating Rural Entrepreneurs," Unilever, http://www.unilever.com/sustainability/casestudies/economic-development/creating-rural-entrepreneurs.aspx.

25. Dasgupta, interview; and Kakkar, interview.

26. Dasgupta, interview.

27. Clayton M. Christensen, Jerome H. Grossman, and Jason Hwang, *The Innovator's Prescription: A Disruptive Solution for Health Care* (New York: McGraw-Hill, 2009), 312–313.

28. "A Thin Blue Line: The History of the Pregnancy Test Kit," National Institutes of Health, http://history.nih.gov/exhibits/thinblueline/timeline.html#pre.

29. Jon Cohen, *Coming to Term: Uncovering the Truth About Miscarriage* (Boston: Houghton Mifflin, 2005), 28–29.

30. "A Thin Blue Line: The History of the Pregnancy Test Kit."

31. These basic archetypes are outlined in both Charles B. Stabell and Øystein Fjeldstad, "Configuring Value for Competitive Advantage:

On Chains, Shops, and Networks," *Strategic Management Journal* (May 1998), 413–437; and Geoffrey A. Moore, "Strategy and Your Stronger Hand," *Harvard Business Review*, December 2005, 62–72.

32. This general framework is addressed by Øystein Fjeldstad and Geoffrey Moore but with some difference in language, as Fjeldstad uses the term *solution shops* while Moore prefers *complex operations*.

33. In describing this framework, Fjeldstad, Moore, and Christensen show a slight variation in language. Fjeldstad uses the term *value chains*, while Christensen prefers *value-adding process*, and Moore employs the terms *volume operations*.

34. Steve Wunker, "Get the Job Done," *Strategy & Innovation* 3, no. 4 (July/August 2005): 11–13.

35. Christensen, Grossman, and Hwang, *The Innovator's Prescription*, 166.

36. Joseph L. Bower and Clark Gilbert, "Pandesic: The Challenges of a New Business Venture (A)," Case 9-399-129 (Boston: Harvard Business School, 1999), and Joseph L. Bower and Clark Gilbert, "Pandesic: The Challenges of a New Business Venture (B)," Case 9-399-130 (Boston: Harvard Business School, 1999).

37. Clayton Christensen and Michael Raynor, "How to Pick Managers for Disruptive Growth," *Harvard Business School Working Knowledge*, October 13, 2003.

Chapter 5

1. Peter J. Williamson and Ming Zeng, "Value-for-Money Strategies for Recessionary Times," *Harvard Business Review*, March 2009, 66–74.

2. Clayton M. Christensen, *The Innovator's Dilemma: When New Technologies Cause Great Firms to Fail* (Boston: Harvard Business School Press, 1997), 24.

3. Ibid., 87–93.

4. Internal research conducted by the author and Innosight in an analysis of approximately 350 different business model innovations.

5. Certain assumptions need to be made before you can get 100 miles out of a battery—this distance means shortened life cycles, as you have to fully charge and drain a battery to achieve this distance today.

6. Shai Agassi, "A Moment of Transfiguration," address given at NDN conference in Washington, D.C., March 12, 2008.

7. Shai Agassi, "A Bold Green Plan," address given at *Fortune's* "Brainstorm: GREEN" conference, Pasadena, CA, April 21, 2008.

8. Agassi, "A Moment of Transfiguration."

9. Shai Agassi, interview by author, tape recording from phone interview, June 11, 2009.

10. Ibid.

11. Shai Agassi, interview by Kristian Steenstrup, February 2009, www.gartner.com/research/fellows/asset_221489_1176.jsp.

12. Agassi, "A Bold Green Plan."

13. Ibid.

14. Shai Agassi, "Shai Agassi's Bold Plan for Electric Cars," address given at TED event in Long Beach, CA, February 2009.

15. Agassi, "A Bold Green Plan."

16. In the months that followed its first announced partnership with Israel, Better Place announced partnership arrangements with Ontario, Australia, Hawaii, and the City of San Francisco.

17. Agassi, "A Bold Green Plan."

Chapter 6

1. The following case study comes from an actual project undertaken by Innosight, although company names have been changed for purposes of confidentiality.

2. Or, if you must start with an existing product, the question is not, "What do you need from my product?" but rather, "What is my product for, and is it the best way to do that job?"

3. Clayton M. Christensen and Michael E. Raynor, *The Innovator's Solution: Creating and Sustaining Successful Growth* (Boston: Harvard Business School Press, 2003), 75–79.

4. Scott Anthony, Mark W. Johnson, Joseph V. Sinfield, and Elizabeth J. Altman, *The Innovator's Guide to Growth: Putting Disruptive Innovation to Work* (Boston: Harvard Business Press, 2008), chapter 4.

5. Clive Thompson, "Batteries Not Included," *New York Times*, April 16, 2009; and Daniel Roth, "Driven: Shai Agassi's Audacious Plan to Put Electric Cars on the Road," *Wired*, August 18, 2008.

6. "Zara, a Spanish Success Story," CNN.com, June 15, 2001, http://edition.cnn.com/BUSINESS/programs/yourbusiness/stories2001/zara/.

7. Miguel Helft, "Fashion Fast Forward," *Business 2.0*, May 2002.

8. Nirmalya Kumar, "Zara: Spanish Season," *Businessworld*, October 2005, http://www.businessworld.in/index.php/Spanish-season.html.

9. Max Chafkin, "The Customer Is the Company," *Inc.*, June 2008.

10. Ibid.

11. Joseph V. Sinfield, E. S. Calder, S. Colson, and B. McConnell, "Developing a Competency in Business Model Innovation," *International Journal of Innovation Management*, in review.

12. I am indebted to Rita McGrath and Ian MacMillan for their elegant formulation of the reverse income statement. See Rita Gunther McGrath and Ian C. MacMillan, *The Entrepreneurial Mindset: Strategies for Continuously Creating Opportunity in an Age of Uncertainty* (Boston: Harvard Business School Press, 2000).

13. Pankaj Ghemawat and José Luis Nueno, "Zara: Fast Fashion," Case 9-703-497 (Boston: Harvard Business School Publishing, 2003), 9.

Chapter 7

1. From a lecture given by David Garvin on behalf of Intel's NBI Group on February 18, 2008, at the Harvard Business School.

2. Rita Gunther McGrath and Ian C. MacMillan, "Discovery-Driven Planning," *Harvard Business Review*, July–August 1995, 44–54.

3. Scott Cook, as quoted in "A Formula for Failure," *BusinessWeek* Playbook: Best Practices, http://www.businessweek.com/playbook/06/0628_1.htm.

4. Scott Cook, comments given at "Meeting the Growth Imperative" forum, Boston, August 7, 2008.

5. Ibid.

6. Scott Anthony, Mark W. Johnson, Joseph V. Sinfield, and Elizabeth J. Altman, *The Innovator's Guide to Growth: Putting Disruptive Innovation to Work* (Boston: Harvard Business Press, 2008), 149.

7. Reed Hastings, comments given at "Meeting the Growth Imperative" forum, Boston, August 7, 2008.

8. Rigas Donganis, *The Airline Business in the Twenty-First Century* (London: Routledge, 2001), 132.

9. Vijay Govindarajan and Julie B. Lang, "Southwest Airlines Corporation," Case 2-0012 (Hanover, NH: Tuck School of Business at Dartmouth, 2002), 1–2.

10. "The Institutional Yes: An Interview with Jeff Bezos," *Harvard Business Review*, October 2007, 74–82.

11. Pankaj Ghemawat and José Luis Nueno, "Zara: Fast Fashion," Case 9-703-497 (Boston: Harvard Business School Publishing, 2003), 15.

12. Ibid.

13. Inditex spokesperson for Zara, interview by the author, tape recording from phone interview, May 27, 2008.

14. Krishnendu Dasgupta and Sanjiv Kakkar, interviews by author, tape recording from phone interview, July 2, 2008, and June 24, 2008.

15. V. Kasturi Rangan and Rohithari Rajan, "Unilever in India: Hindustan Lever's Project Shakti—Marketing FMCG to the Rural Consumer," Case 9-505-056 (Boston: Harvard Business School Publishing, 2002), 14.

16. Terry Kelly, comments given at "Meeting the Growth Imperative" forum, Boston, August 7, 2008.

17. Sheets, interview.

18. Brad Anderson, comments given at "Meeting the Growth Imperative" forum, Boston, August 3, 2007.

19. Ronald N. Ashkenas and Suzanne C. Francis, "Integration Managers: Special Leaders for Special Times," *Harvard Business Review*, November–December 2000, 108–116; and Larry Selden and Geoffrey Colvin, "M&A Needn't Be a Loser's Game," *Harvard Business Review*, June 2003, 70–79.

20. John Deighton, "How Snapple Got Its Juice Back," *Harvard Business Review*, January 2002, 47–53.

21. Matt Vela, "Electronic Arts 2.0," *BusinessWeek*, October 29, 2007.

22. Christian Nutt and Brandon Boyer, "DICE Keynote: EA's Riccitiello on a New Future for Publishing," *Gamasutra*, February 8, 2008, http://www.gamasutra.com/php-bin/news_index.php?story=17313.

23. Seth Schiesel, "A Company Looks to Its Creative Side to Regain What It Had Lost," *New York Times*, February 19, 2008.

24. Brad Anderson, comments given at "Meeting the Growth Imperative," Boston, August 3, 2007.

25. Don Tapscott and Anthony D. Williams, *Wikinomics: How Mass Collaboration Changes Everything* (New York: Portfolio, 2006), 239.

26. Vijay Govindarajan and Chris Trimble, *Ten Rules for Strategic Innovators: From Idea to Execution* (Boston: Harvard Business School Press, 2005), 6.

Chapter 8

1. Steve Sasson, "PluggedIn: A Blog about Kodak Products and Customers," October 16, 2007, http://stevesasson.pluggedin.kodak.com/default.asp?item=687843.

2. Claudia H. Deutsch, "At Kodak, Some Old Things Are New Again," *New York Times*, May 2, 2008.

3. Ibid.

4. W. Blair Haworth, *The Bradley and How It Got That Way: Technology, Institutions, and the Problem of Mechanized Infantry in the United States Army* (Westport, CT: Greenwood Press, 1999), 28, 78.

5. From the film *The Pentagon Wars*, as cited in Michael A. Prospero, "Build an Army for Your Ideas," *Fast Company*, June, 2006.

6. Marco Meyrat, interview by author, tape recording from phone interview, June 17, 2008.

7. Clayton M. Christensen, "Hewlett-Packard: The Flight of the Kittyhawk (A)," Case 9-606-088 (Boston: Harvard Business School Publishing, 2006).

8. Meyrat, interview.

9. Clayton M. Christensen, Stephen P. Kaufman, and Willy C. Shih, "Innovation Killers: How Financial Tools Destroy Your Capacity to Do New Things," *Harvard Business Review*, January 2008, 98–105.

10. Steven Kerr, "On the Folly of Rewarding A, While Hoping for B," *Academy of Management Journal* 18, no. 4 (December 1975): 769–783.

11. Richard Foster and Sarah Kaplan, *Creative Destruction: Why Companies That Are Built to Last Underperform the Market—and How to Successfully Transform Them* (New York: Currency, 2001), 162.

12. Alfred D. Chandler, *Strategy and Structure: Chapters in the History of the American Industrial Enterprise* (Cambridge, MA: MIT Press, 1990), 14.

13. Joseph L. Bower and Clark G. Gilbert, "How Managers' Everyday Decisions Create—or Destroy—Your Company's Strategy," *Harvard Business Review*, February 2007, 72–79.

14. "The Institutional Yes: An Interview with Jeff Bezos," *Harvard Business Review*, October 2007, 74–82.

Epilogue

1. Peter F. Drucker, "The Theory of the Business," *Harvard Business Review*, September–October 1994, 95–104.

2. Richard Foster and Sarah Kaplan, *Creative Destruction: Why Companies That Are Built to Last Underperform the Market—and How to Successfully Transform Them* (New York: Currency, 2001), 13; and Innosight and Dick Foster internal research derived from an aggregate of sources including Bloomberg.

3. Amazon.com, Inc., "2002 Annual Report," and "2008 Annual Report."

4. "How Amazon Opens Up and Cleans Up," *BusinessWeek* "Special Report: Will Web Services Click?" June 24, 2003.

5. Amazon.com, Inc., "Q4 2007 Financial Results," January 30, 2008.

6. Although Amazon does not disclose sales figures, Citigroup analyst Mark Mahaney has projected that 2008 Kindle sales were

approximately 500,000, as noted in Douglas MacMillan, "Amazon Kindle 2: No iPod for Books," *BusinessWeek*, February 10, 2009.

7. Jeff Bezos, interview by author, tape recording from phone interview, October 27, 2008.

8. Reed Hastings, comments given at Innosight's "Meeting the Growth Imperative" forum, Boston, August 7, 2008.

ACKNOWLEDGMENTS

I have been pondering the question of business models and business model innovation almost since I began Innosight with my friend and colleague Clayton Christensen nearly ten years ago. In a meeting Clay had with former Intel CEO Andy Grove in 1999, Grove rightly pointed out that disruptive threats came inherently not from new technology but from new business models. Since then, we have realized that disruptive innovation and business model innovation were opposite sides of the same coin. But that led to the questions: What really is a business model? and How do you create a truly new one? The words *business model innovation* have been bandied about, particularly since the Internet boom of the late 1990s, but no one had come up with any satisfying framework from which to work.

Then in 2005 my client and good friend Dan Pantaleo, a vice president in Global Communications at SAP AG, asked me to help him identify the most pressing issues that the company's senior clients and executives should be focusing on for the future. We immediately converged on business model innovation as the topic we thought most needed to be better defined and understood. We collaborated for almost two years, deeply researching several companies we deemed business model innovators and holding a series of CEO summits on the topic. The work led ultimately to "Reinventing Your Business Model," the McKinsey Award–winning article in *Harvard Business Review,* which I wrote with Clay Christensen and former SAP CEO Henning Kagermann. Throughout, Dan was an invaluable colleague, always willing to engage deeply in the hard task of understanding the real challenges involved in transformative growth and renewal through business model innovation.

From these early efforts arose many more questions, which led me to write this book. In it, I have attempted to describe business models in a simple framework that can be easily grasped and applied to new business model development. I've then attempted to apply the framework to the cases I've studied firsthand. This research forms the core of the book.

Right now, companies around the world, in both developed and developing countries, are conceiving and implementing innovative new business models. I have sought, through the stories of those I've researched in depth, to bring the power and the possibilities of the business model framework to life. I don't wish to suggest that this framework is the only way to think about business models. Rather, I offer it as a useful lens through which to view your white space as a less-scary place and make the process of conceiving and constructing new business models into a predictable process that can be reliably managed. As such, I hope the framework will be applicable not just to private-sector businesses but also to many other institutions—NGOs, government agencies, defense contractors—that need to respond to changing circumstances or may be frustrated in their attempts to capitalize on new opportunities.

The long journey from conceptualization to writing a book could not have been completed without the help of a host of people.

In addition to Dan Pantaleo of SAP, I am grateful to my coauthor on the HBR article, Henning Kagermann, and to the dedicated support of Herbert Heitmann and Stacy Comes at SAP Global Communications.

Special thanks go to Karl Ronn, John Leikham, and George Glackin at Procter & Gamble, who have given me extensive feedback and guidance on the business model framework over the years. They've been kind enough to engage in hours of spirited dialogue and debate about how to make business models and business model innovation relevant to practitioners.

Scott Cook, chairman of Intuit, provided invaluable input in reviewing versions of both the HBR article and various parts of the manuscript. His comments are always so rich in insight and pushed my thinking tremendously.

Nelson Handel, a delightfully creative and gifted storyteller, helped me enormously in the sometimes mystical task of taking the story out of my head and putting it on paper. Nelson spent countless hours talking with me about the ideas, assisting with the research, doing yeoman's work on the initial drafts, and working with me through innumerable iterations, remaining ever patient and vigilant to make sure we told the story right.

I also would like to extend my deep appreciation to the numerous colleagues who graciously gave of their time to review all or part of the manuscript, whose comments I found invaluable: Vivek Bapat of SAP; Peter Blackman and Dominique Fournier of Infineum; Stefan Bockamp of E.ON AG; Bob Boyd, Ken Disken, and Neil Kacena of Lockheed Martin; Larry Burns and Tony Posawatz of GM; Kim Clark of BYU-Idaho; Roy Davis, Michelle Goodridge, Jack Groppel, Calvin Schmidt, and Harlan Weisman of Johnson & Johnson; Chris Fleck of Citrix Systems; John Gatti of BAE Systems; Hang Chang Chieh of National University of Singapore; Tarun Khanna and Willy Shih of Harvard Business School; Susan Marcinelli of Best Buy; Steve Milunovich of Merrill

Lynch; Steve Spear of MIT; Gary Williams of wRatings Corporation; and Tom Wilkerson of the U.S. Naval Institute. Clement Chen of SAIC and Russ Conser of Shell gave particularly detailed and insightful comments, which significantly advanced my thinking in many parts of the book.

My colleagues at Innosight, each and every one of them, past and present, have taught and continue to teach me every day. Particular thanks go to Josh Suskewicz, who was instrumental early on in the business model research, as well as to former colleagues Alex Leichtman and Lilac Berniker. Alex Slawsby and Jennifer Gaze also provided very helpful research and support. Thoughtful reviews of the manuscript came from Ryan Fisher, Tim Huse, Dave Goulait, and Andy Waldeck. Steve Wunker provided indispensable contributions in the development of early chapter drafts. Ned Calder and Joe Sinfield were very helpful with their contributions in the development of chapter 6, "Designing a New Business Model."

Andrea Ovans provided outstanding editorial contributions. She was ever insistent on stating things precisely and clearly, and I am extremely grateful for her insistence on brevity and preservation of logic through and through. I also greatly appreciate the editorial contributions from Eileen Roche, Janice Evans, and Renee Callahan, for their careful, exacting review of the manuscript, and to Daniel Guidera for his high-quality contributions to the development of all of the graphics. Judi Haviland and HBR's Karen Player also provided a very helpful eye in shaping the graphics.

I'm deeply indebted to my primary editors at Harvard Business Press: former editor Hollis Heimbouch, who got me on my way, having enough faith to sign me on as an author, and Jacque Murphy, a marvelous coach who provided lots of encouragement throughout the process. I'm also grateful to Allison Peter and Ania Wieckowski of the Press for their invariably kind assistance.

I owe a very special thanks to Allen Stoddard. Allen shepherded so many important elements of the manuscript development and peer review process, I really can't commend him enough for his diligence, attention to detail, positive attitude, and willingness to endure long hours to see the book through to completion.

I am especially beholden to my colleagues and fellow Innosight board members Scott Anthony, Matt Eyring, Dick Foster, and Clark Gilbert for their support while I was writing the book and their extremely perceptive reviews of the manuscript. Through all these years they have not only been tremendous colleagues but also great friends.

Clay Christensen's resolute support, his steadfast willingness to listen, and ever astute review of the work mean more than I can ever adequately capture in words. He is a man of supreme intellect, compassion, and humility. He has taught me what it means to give deeply of oneself, and I am forever grateful for all he has done for me personally and professionally.

I owe a tremendous debt to my lifelong mentor and friend Leo S. Tonkin, Esq., who instilled in me the famous words "The unexamined life is not worth living." His guidance along my life's journey has in so many ways large and small influenced my thinking about the world and about matters both professional and personal. His influence permeates this book, and for that I am forever grateful.

My deepest gratitude goes to my family. My children are a constant source of joy and inspire me to be a better person. My wife, Jane, is my greatest champion and best friend. She has been a tremendous source of wisdom and support throughout the research and writing of this book. As a journalist, she has taught me the power of a story well told, helping me sharpen the manuscript and bring it to life. Above all, Jane has taught me the importance of connecting with and caring for others. Her kindness and finely tuned intuition for people, and truth, have made my life richer and sweeter than I could have ever imagined.

INDEX

Note: Page numbers followed by *f* refer to figures; numbers followed by *t* refer to tables.

ABOUT THE AUTHOR

Mark Johnson is chairman of Innosight, a strategic innovation consulting and investing company with offices in Massachusetts, Singapore, and India, which he cofounded with Harvard Business School professor Clayton M. Christensen. He has consulted to Global 1,000 and start-up companies in a wide range of industries—including health care, aerospace/defense, enterprise IT, energy, automotive, and consumer packaged goods—and has advised Singapore's government on innovation and entrepreneurship.

Mark's most recent work has focused on helping companies envision and create new growth, manage transformation, and achieve renewal through business model innovation. This work is the subject of the McKinsey award–winning *Harvard Business Review* article, "Reinventing Your Business Model," coauthored by Clayton Christensen and Henning Kagermann. Mark also coauthored *The Innovator's Guide to Growth* (Harvard Business Press, 2008) and has published articles in the *Sloan Management Review*, *Advertising Age*, and *National Defense*.

Prior to cofounding Innosight, Mark was a consultant at Booz Allen Hamilton, where he advised clients on managing innovation and implementing comprehensive change programs. Before that, he served as a nuclear power–trained surface warfare officer in the U. S. Navy in the first Gulf War.

Mark received an MBA from Harvard Business School, a master's degree in civil engineering and engineering mechanics from Columbia University, and a bachelor's degree with distinction in aerospace engineering from the United States Naval Academy. He currently serves on the board of the U.S. Naval Institute.

Mark, his wife, Jane Clayson Johnson, and their children live in Belmont, Massachusetts.